Building Multiplayer Games in Unity

Using Mirror Networking

Dylan Engelbrecht

Apress®

Building Multiplayer Games in Unity: Using Mirror Networking

Dylan Engelbrecht
Johannesburg, South Africa

ISBN-13 (pbk): 978-1-4842-7473-6   ISBN-13 (electronic): 978-1-4842-7474-3
https://doi.org/10.1007/978-1-4842-7474-3

Managing Director, Apress Media LLC: Welmoed Spahr
Acquisitions Editor: Spandana Chatterjee
Development Editor: Laura Berendson
Coordinating Editor: Shrikant Vishwakarma

Cover designed by eStudioCalamar

Cover image designed by Pexels

Distributed to the book trade worldwide by Springer Science+Business Media LLC, 1 New York Plaza, Suite 4600, New York, NY 10004. Phone 1-800-SPRINGER, fax (201) 348-4505, e-mail orders-ny@springer-sbm.com, or visit www.springeronline.com. Apress Media, LLC is a California LLC and the sole member (owner) is Springer Science + Business Media Finance Inc (SSBM Finance Inc). SSBM Finance Inc is a **Delaware** corporation.

For information on translations, please e-mail booktranslations@springernature.com; for reprint, paperback, or audio rights, please e-mail bookpermissions@springernature.com, or visit http://www.apress.com/rights-permissions.

Apress titles may be purchased in bulk for academic, corporate, or promotional use. eBook versions and licenses are also available for most titles. For more information, reference our Print and eBook Bulk Sales web page at http://www.apress.com/bulk-sales.

Any source code or other supplementary material referenced by the author in this book is available to readers on GitHub via the book's product page, located at www.apress.com/978-1-4842-7473-6. For more detailed information, please visit http://www.apress.com/source-code.

Printed on acid-free paper

*"The pursuit of mastery is an endless journey,
but those who persevere etch their names in history."*

—*Riot Games*

Table of Contents

About the Author

Dylan Engelbrecht is a Unity specialist. Born and raised in South Africa, he has worked at the top enterprise VR development studio in the country, and he's currently working at the largest game development studio on the continent. He has in-depth knowledge of commercial and enterprise game development, with work showcased by invite at Comic Con Africa and rAge Expo. He is an avid gamer who enjoys immersive experiences and real-time strategy games.

About the Technical Reviewer

 **Deepak Jadhav** is a game developer based in Bonn, Germany. He received his bachelor's in Computer Technology and master's in Game Programming and Project Management. Deepak has been involved in developing games on multiple platforms such as mobiles, console, and PC. He has a strong background in C# and C++ as well as years of experience in using Unity, Unreal Engine for Game Development, Augmented Reality, Mixed Reality, and Virtual Reality.

CHAPTER 1

A Brief Introduction

Content is king, but a king is nothing without the people. The same applies to games. You could create all of the world's content and walk your new land like a king – but it would still feel like it's missing something. Humans are social creatures, craving interaction and shared experiences. We're fascinated by new ways of experiencing, and linear, single-player experiences are great, but they can feel empty and soulless if not done perfectly.

Welcome to *Building Multiplayer Games in Unity Using Mirror Networking*, where I'll take you on a deep dive into multiplayer with Unity3D. We'll use Mirror Networking to bring your players together, creating the ultimate shared experience. Learn the fundamentals of RPC/Command multiplayer architecture, and dig deeper into networking and data persistence to achieve scalable, highly performant, large-scale multiplayer.

You'll learn to develop multiplayer games using Unity within a commercial or enterprise environment. We'll take a look behind the scenes at what makes multiplayer games tick. Explore how you can utilize different authoritative structures to best suit your needs. We'll also look into scaling your architecture and explore industry-leading methods of deploying your game to the masses.

You'll form a solid understanding of valuable networking principles and boost your game development career. Finally, we'll wrap up with some advice from leading experts who've deployed the games that you love and play. These experts will shed light on past mistakes and provide valuable advice for your next project.

© Dylan Engelbrecht 2022
D. Engelbrecht, *Building Multiplayer Games in Unity*, https://doi.org/10.1007/978-1-4842-7474-3_1

Why Multiplayer?

Multiplayer, used right, can add a certain depth to a game that we cannot achieve otherwise. I'm not implying that you should make every game multiplayer. Certain games do indeed feel better as a single-player experience if done right. So, it's essential to look at what your product has to offer, its downfalls, and what multiplayer can give or take from the player experience.

Benefits of Multiplayer

Let's explore some of the benefits of multiplayer:

- **It adds a new dimension to how players interact with your product** - Multiplayer allows players to interact with the experience you've designed and with each other. Creating a whole new dimension for how players interact with your product has the potential to be extremely rewarding.

- **Multiplayer games boost social interaction, resulting in improved user retention** - Humans are social creatures of habit. We thrive on interacting with other people. For some, this can be more challenging due to social anxiety. However, games have a unique way of breaking down this barrier, allowing your players to form meaningful friendships. Those friendships in themselves add new reasons for your players to keep coming back, resulting in improved player retention.

- **Multiplayer begets competition and cooperation** - Competition is a fundamental trait amplified through games. Healthy competition can encourage more extended use of your product by your players, resulting in more monetization opportunities. At the same time, depending on game design, multiplayer brings cooperation where players should work as a team and which helps engaging players in a creative way.

- **More effective analytics and player behavioral data** - Games as a service allow us more flexibility in collecting player behavioral data and analytics that we can use to improve our product. This behavioral data becomes exponentially more powerful in enterprise environments, where you have more consent to user data.

- **Community engagement** - Multiplayer games are a great source of content for streamers and content creators. This influencer-driven marketing will prove invaluable in driving your community engagement and offering new forms of monetization.

Caveats of Multiplayer

Multiplayer offers many benefits, but it does have some caveats that you should be aware of when deciding to build or convert your existing product into a multiplayer game:

- **Not all games make for an excellent multiplayer experience** - Some games are just better as a single-player experience. If done incorrectly, multiplayer can take more away from a game than it can give, which is especially prevalent in very story-driven games, where the narrative revolves around the player.

- **Multiplayer service life expectancy** - If you're providing your product as a service, you'll need to host the dedicated servers yourself. Product as a service brings up a caveat of multiplayer games that rely on the developer to host the game, and that's the multiplayer service life expectancy. Most multiplayer games that developers host will not run indefinitely. Eventually, developers will shut the servers down. Mitigate service life expectancy by evolving your product to keep pace with the market or finally giving your players the ability to host private servers.

- **Competition begets toxicity** - The same competition that encourages more use of your product can also decay into toxicity if left unchecked. This decay could result in users leaving or negative publicity. So how do we mitigate this risk? Let's look at the next point.

- **Moderation of user-interactive spaces** - To prevent your community's decay, you'll need to look into moderation options to ensure that your community isn't creating a negative experience for new users.

The Options of Multiplayer in Unity

There are several options available to us when creating multiplayer games with Unity. Each of these options has various pros, cons, and outright limitations. So it's critical to evaluate your game's needs and decide what you're willing to sacrifice. Let's have a look at Figure 1-1 to compare a few of the top networking solutions.

	Unity HLAPI	Unity MLAPI	Mirror	PUN	DarkRift 2	DOTSNET
Pricing	Free	Free	Free	$0.30 / PCU	Free & Paid	Paid
Pricing Structure	-	-	-	Monthly	Once	Once
Status	Deprecated	In Development	Active	Active	Active	Active
Product Type	Standalone	Standalone	Standalone	Service	Standalone	Standalone
Single Game CCU	~32	~64	~500+	~8	~1000+	~1000+
CCU License Limit	None	None	None	Package Dependant	None	None
Difficulty	Easy	-	Easy	Easy	Difficult	Difficult
Support	No	-	Community	Community & Premium	Community & Premium	Community

Figure 1-1. *A comparison chart with various Unity networking solutions and frameworks*

Note   Single-game CCU (Concurrent Users on the same game server at the same time) is highly dependent on your game's architecture and coding.

So, why not develop a multiplayer game in Unity using Unity's built-in HLAPI? Well, that's what you'd expect. Unity has a networking framework, called UNet, and a big part of UNet is the HLAPI or High-Level Application Programming Interface. However, the Unity HLAPI is deprecated, and you really should avoid it for any new projects. It also has several limitations, preventing it from being a good, scalable solution. Unity has promised us a new networking framework. Unity released the initial public version of their new multiplayer framework, called MLAPI, in March 2021. Many of the concepts you'll learn in this book will also apply to the MLAPI, as they're all loosely based around the same source code and architecture.

Why Mirror?

So, if there are so many networking options available, then why choose Mirror? Well, Mirror has built-in support for switching out the transport layer, which removes a lot of the limitations in other networking solutions, namely, how many concurrent players we can get into a single instance. Mirror is also free and relatively easy to use and implement, with a massive supportive community that will gladly assist you with any problems or questions.

Prerequisites and Resources

To follow along with this book, you'll need the following tools, source code, and knowledge.

PREREQUISITES AND RESOURCES

- Be experienced in C#, there will be a lot of coding involved, and C# experience is required if you'd like to follow along with this book.

- Proficient in Unity, you should have a solid understanding of Unity and its design patterns.

- Unity3D, in this book I'll be using Unity 2020.3 LTS which you can download from Unity Hub.

- Mirror, the networking framework that we'll be using throughout this book. You can get the latest build from the Unity Asset Store.

- KCP, which you can download from the mirror website, `https://mirror-networking.com/transports/`.

- An IDE, such as Visual Studio. My preferred IDE is JetBrains Rider.

- Wireshark, which you can download and install from `www.wireshark.org/download.html`.

- Optionally, an AWS free tier account, which you can sign up for at `https://aws.amazon.com/free/`.

Did you know?   Mirror was created to replace a deprecated UNet and was originally released October 2018.

Summary

In this chapter, we explored what multiplayer can offer your game or product, as well as the caveats that come with multiplayer game development. We explored what our options are when developing a multiplayer game and got a brief introduction to who I am and what you'll be learning in this book.

In the next chapter, we'll tackle the foundational elements of networking, to understand exactly how data travels around the world.

CHAPTER 2

The Messenger Pigeon, Packets, and a Trip Around the World

Before we begin creating multiplayer games using one of the many provided APIs, it's crucial to understand how computers communicate with each other. Understanding how computers communicate will allow us to improve network performance and weed out pesky bugs. In this chapter, we'll be touching on the history of computer networking and discussing the fundamental principles that enable computers to communicate.

Introduction to Networking

A network in computer terminology, by definition, is a group of computers or devices that communicate using a shared communication protocol. The two primary protocols that we'll be discussing for game development are TCP and UDP. These two standard protocols are what allow devices to communicate with one another in a common language.

D. Engelbrecht, *Building Multiplayer Games in Unity*, https://doi.org/10.1007/978-1-4842-7474-3_2

A Brief History of Networking

It's crucial to understand the importance of standardized protocols in computer networking. Before the Open Systems Interconnection Model, or OSI model, was created in 1978 by French computer scientist Hubert Zimmerman, computer networking was largely unstandardized. The lack of standardization meant that computer networking, in large part, was limited to massive government-funded contracts or limited to vendor-specific standards. Essentially, computers all spoke different languages to one another, without a common tongue. The world needed a set standard to follow, a universal language.

The first significant attempt at this standardization, or common tongue, was conceived. The OSI model was a massive industry undertaking, attempting to persuade industry participants to agree on common networking standards to allow for multi-vendor interoperability. The seven-layer OSI model provided a conceptual framework for engineers to build around, allowing devices to communicate easily with one another, regardless of vendor, internal structure, or technology.

Now, the OSI model itself is obsolete for the most part, as it never gained the popularity that it needed to achieve its goal. However, it did highlight the dire need for a standardized approach to networking. It's worth noting that despite the OSI model not gaining the popularity that it needed, we still use the OSI model today for reference and teaching.

During roughly the same period, two scientists developed another set of protocols that would become what OSI should have been. These two scientists, Vinton Gray "Vint" Cerf and Robert Kahn, would later be known as "The fathers of the Internet." Robert Kahn was hired in 1972 by Lawrence Roberts, the program manager of the Information Processing Techniques Office (IPTO), a Defense Advanced Research Projects Agency (DARPA) branch of the US Department of Defense. While working at IPTO, Robert Kahn started a project to establish a ground-based radio packet network. He faced similar challenges that the industry was facing. He realized a need to develop an open architecture model that would allow networks to communicate, regardless of hardware and software configuration. Robert Kahn set forth to create such a model and proposed four critical goals for designing the model. This model would later become known as the Transmission Control Protocol (TCP). Interestingly, early versions of the technology had the same abbreviation as its modern counterpart but stood for Transmission Control Program.

The four initial goals for TCP were as follows:

- **Intercommunication** - Any network should communicate with another network, regardless of hardware or software configuration, through a gateway.

- **Robust** - No internal changes would have to be made to a network to connect to another network.

- **Distributed** - The protocol should allow for a distributed network with no central network administration or control.

- **Error handling and recovery** - The protocol should be able to detect lost packets and retransmit them.

In 1973, Vinton Gray joined Robert Kahn on the project, where the two would work together on TCP. Later, in May 1974, Vinton and Robert wrote a paper, published by the Institute of Electrical and Electronics Engineers (IEEE), describing their internetworking protocol for sharing resources using packet switching among network nodes. Later, this work resulted in the Internet Protocol (IP) Suite.

And in March 1982, the US Department of Defense declared TCP/IP as the standard for all military computer networking. Later, in 1985, the Internet Architecture Board (IAB) held a three-day workshop on TCP/IP for the computer industry, promoting the protocol and its eventual commercial use, finally achieving the OSI model's original goal.

While Vinton and Robert were cementing their technology in the industry, another notable scientist appeared in the early 1980s, a computer scientist named David Patrick Reed. David developed a protocol called the User Datagram Protocol (UDP). UDP is an alternative transport layer protocol designed with simplicity in mind. Created on top of the Internet Protocol Suite, it provides incredible speed while transmitting packets over the network, albeit sacrificing TCP's error correction and handling and reliability.

Understanding Packets

Now that we know why TCP and UDP were created, let's dive into the how. A packet is a formatted unit of data, generally a part of a larger message. We can break this packet down further into control information and a payload. The control information defines the packet's information, for example, where it needs to go, where it came from, and perhaps even the packet's order. The payload is typically the user data.

Typically, in a multiplayer game, if we have a player named Lucy and a player named John, they will be sharing packets of data among one another to keep the state of the game synced. If Lucy moves five units north, she'll send a data packet with a payload representing that movement. John then receives the packet and interprets the payload. He can then see that Lucy moved five units North and update his visual representation of Lucy to move five units North.

In many cases, the various multiplayer tools and APIs available for Unity will allow you to share that information between Lucy and John without ever seeing the packet directly, so it almost becomes easy to forget that they exist, especially for newcomers to multiplayer. However, that's no reason to downplay the importance of packets. Understanding how packets are structured and how your data affects packets is vital to create scalable, smooth, multiplayer experiences.

Typically, when creating a multiplayer game, you'll be using either TCP or UDP or a combination of both. TCP and UDP each have their strengths and weaknesses, determining where you use them based on your project's individual needs.

Comparing TCP and UDP		
	TCP	**UDP**
Usage	Where data transmission needs to be reliable, and resistant to errors.	Where data transmission needs to be very fast and you don't really care about the reliability of the target receiving your packets.
Connection	Connection-Focused	Connectionless
Reliability	Reliable	Unreliable
Ordering	Ordered	Un-ordererd
Error Checking	Supports Error Checking	None
Acknowledgment	Yes	No
Speed	Slow in comparison to UDP	Very fast comparison to TCP
Overhead	Medium	Very Low
Header Size	20-60 Bytes	8 Bytes
Targeting	Single Target	Supports Multicast
Security	High in comparison to UDP	Low in comparison to TCP
Game Use-Cases	Game Chat & Social Features	Replicating User Actions and Time-critical data

Figure 2-1. *The figure is comparing the core differences between TCP and UDP*

A Look at TCP Packets

Let's take a look at Figure 2-1. Here, we can see that TCP is a reliable protocol that allows us to transmit ordered data from A to B securely. What exactly does that mean? Well, a TCP connection involves each party confirming or acknowledging the receipt of a data packet. Let's look at Lucy and John for another analogy and create an extreme situation to visualize data flow.

We'll use Figure 2-2 for reference, which represents how a TCP packet looks.

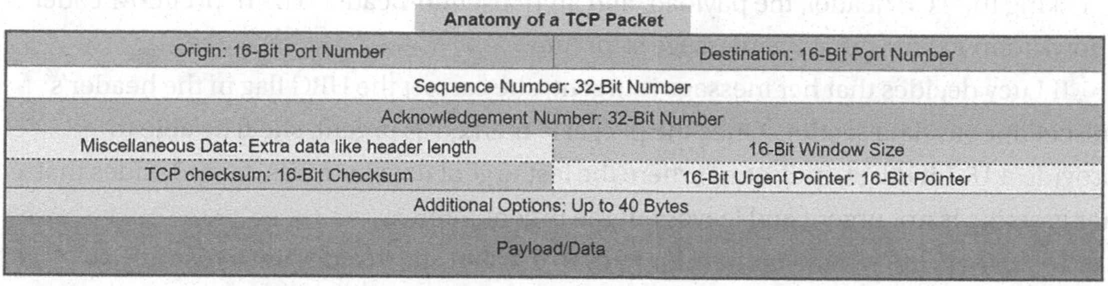

Anatomy of a TCP Packet			
Origin: 16-Bit Port Number		Destination: 16-Bit Port Number	
Sequence Number: 32-Bit Number			
Acknowledgement Number: 32-Bit Number			
Miscellaneous Data: Extra data like header length		16-Bit Window Size	
TCP checksum: 16-Bit Checksum		16-Bit Urgent Pointer: 16-Bit Pointer	
Additional Options: Up to 40 Bytes			
Payload/Data			

Figure 2-2. *This figure breaks down the structure of a TCP packet*

Firstly, notice how there is an optional section that allows for up to 40 bytes of data? The additional options are why the header can be between 20 and 60 bytes long. Secondly, see how the destination only includes a port number and no IP address? That's because TCP doesn't know or care about IP addresses. It is solely responsible for transmitting application-level data from application to application reliably. It's the job of the Internet Protocol to send the packet between devices. Let's put ourselves in the shoes of TCP for the sake of our analogy; we don't know anything about IP addresses or how the data gets from Lucy to John. We only care that Lucy and John speak the same language. They're both using TCP to communicate.

Firstly, Lucy will need to greet John. TCP is a connection-oriented, byte stream service with reliability. Connection-oriented means that two applications using TCP must first establish a connection before exchanging data. Once Lucy has greeted John, she can now start speaking to him. So, she puts together a packet of data for John. The origin is her mouth, and the destination is John's ears. The sequence then determines the order of the message, preventing John from hearing "Goodbye" before "Hello!"

Next, Lucy smiles while talking to indicate intent. The miscellaneous data within a packet contains various little pieces of information about the packet. These small pieces of information are called flags and provide information about the packet, such as intent. Lucy then indicates how much she's willing to stay and listen to John's response. The window part of the TCP packet represents the size of the receive window, which specifies the number of bytes that this segment's sender is willing to receive at any point in time.

Lucy then puts together a checksum, a data piece that will allow John to know that he heard Lucy correctly. The 16-bit checksum field of the TCP packet gets used for error-checking the TCP header, the payload, and an IP pseudo-header. The IP pseudo-header allows John to know that the message is for him.

If Lucy decides that her message is urgent, she can set the URG flag in the header's miscellaneous data section. Once the packet is marked as urgent, she'll be able to provide a 16-bit offset, indicating where the last urgent data byte was. Lucy decides that her greeting is not urgent and leaves out the urgent pointer.

Next, there are several options for Lucy to use, but she decides not to use any as those go outside the scope of this explanation. Finally, Lucy pads the rest of her headers with 0s until her header ends, and data begins on a 32-bit boundary.

Finally, Lucy adds data to her TCP packet, "Hello! How are you?" John hears Lucy's message and can understand it.

A Look at UDP packets

Next up, we have UDP packets. The User Datagram Protocol is connectionless, which may seem confusing at first. But, we should remember that UDP is not responsible for the actual transmission of the packet. UDP is simply a protocol for us to transmit data through the Internet protocol. However, unlike TCP, it doesn't care about who the recipient is. Unlike TCP, UDP does not require a connection to the destination.

Let's take a look at the anatomy of a UDP packet (Figure 2-3).

Anatomy of a UDP Packet	
Source Port: 16 Bit Number	Destination Port: 16 Bit Number
Length: 16 Bit	Checksum: Optional 16 Bit Field
Payload/Data	

Figure 2-3. *The figure showcases a UDP packet*

The first thing we notice about UDP packets is that they're tiny compared to TCP packets. UDP packet headers are a measly 8 bytes. Compare this to the potentially 60 bytes of header data in a TCP packet in a worst-case scenario. Now, you might be thinking that 60 bytes still seems small. What about my 200Mbps fiber connection at home? Sure, a single 60-byte packet will go unnoticed by your Internet connection, but we need to think in terms of scale.

What if you're dealing with 60 packets a second? Okay, so we're up to 3.6KB/s, big deal, right? Game server with 100 connected players? 360KB/s. Well, even that doesn't sound so bad, right? Well, that's 360KB/s on headers alone. The exact amount of packets over UDP would be 48KB/s in comparison. That's a massive 87% improvement. Keep this in mind for later when we discuss the importance of keeping your packets small. When we work with multiplayer code, it's vital to put yourself into a scalability mindset.

Let's use a similar analogy to what we used with TCP to see the difference between TCP and UDP. This time, Lucy is giving a presentation in front of hundreds of guests at a major event. The source is once again her mouth, with the destination being everyone's ears. However, this time, Lucy is giving a presentation; she doesn't know who the guests are. Instead, she's able to broadcast to anyone who can hear her in the room. She shares her presentation, and John, who is one of the guests, hears her presentation. Lucy doesn't care or even know that John is there or if he can listen to her presentation. This fast-paced transfer of data is ideal in situations where you need to relay a lot of information while having many listeners. Sure, John might have missed a word here and there, but he hears enough of the presentation to make sense of it.

How Packets of Data Get Transported Around the World

So, we understand that packets are a storage container for data transported through the transport layer, but we haven't spoken much about how we send the data across the world. So in this section, I'll be going into more detail on how networks communicate. We'll discuss how that packet of yours will travel from your game server to your game clients.

TCP/IP Model

I briefly introduced the OSI model and how it attempted to standardize networking. Now, let's have an in-depth look at the TCP/IP Model. TCP/IP is an extensive suite of protocols named after its two most important members. It, much like the OSI model, is a conceptual framework. However, unlike the OSI model's seven layers, the TCP/IP Model has only five layers.

Let's take a look at Figure 2-4.

	The TCP/IP Model	Protocol Data Unit	TCP/IP Protocols					Purpose
5	Application	Data	HTTP	FTP	Telnet	SMTP	DNS	Application
4	Transport Layer	Segments	TCP			UDP		
3	Network Layer	Packets	IPv4		IPv6	ARP		Data Flow
2	Data Link Layer	Frames	IEEE 802 Protocol Family					
1	Physical Layer	Bits	None					

Figure 2-4. *A diagram illustrating the five-layer TCP/IP Model and its various protocols for data transmission over the network*

The TCP/IP Model splits into five different layers. These five layers are the following:

- **The application layer** - This layer is responsible for creating and interpreting data. In multiplayer games, this will be the actual game or game server's job. The game and game server fall within the application layer. Data within the application layer could be a variable called *"playerHealth"* as an example. The protocol data unit of the application layer is simply known as data. The application layer includes HTTP protocols outside of game development, which your web browser uses to display websites. Its purpose is to be used by applications running on devices.

- **The transport layer** - This layer is responsible for converting our data into either TCP or UDP segments, depending on the transport layer that we're using. Transport layer packets are known as segments within the TCP/IP Model. These "segments" are the protocol data unit of the transport layer. These transport layer packets, or segments, are what we covered when looking at TCP and UDP packets. The main protocols used by the transport layer are TCP and UDP.

- **The network layer** - This layer is responsible for the segment-packet conversion. The network layer is where our segments (transport layer packets) are converted into packets and sent to our network adapter. Packets are the protocol data unit within the network layer. The most used protocols within the network layer are IPv4 and the Address Resolution Protocol (ARP).

- **The data-link layer** - This is where our packets get converted from packets to frames. Frames are essentially just another type of data container, forming the protocol data unit of the data-link layer.

- **The physical layer** - This layer is responsible for using frames and transmitting them as bits over the network, between devices. Bits are the protocol data unit of the physical layer. The most important layers to understand in game development are the application and transport layers. However, it is crucial to understand the other layers, too, as this will help significantly with debugging.

IPv4 – Internet Protocol Version 4

IPv4 is the fourth version of the Internet Protocol. It's a network layer protocol responsible for internetworking, the practice of interconnecting multiple computer networks. It's one of the main protocols that essentially enables the Internet. IPv4 uses logical addressing and routing to allow the delivery of packets across the living room or past the ocean. IPv4 was originally deployed for production between 1982 and 1983, yet it is still responsible for routing the large majority of Internet traffic today.

The protocol itself isn't perfect, however. When it was originally created, no one could ever anticipate what it would become. IPv4 is the protocol that started the Internet. Originally, the Internet was simply a playground for academics; no one could have anticipated the global reach and adoption. As such, when IPv4 was created, there was no expected need for a large addressing space, so a 32-bit addressing system was created.

The reason behind a 32-bit addressing space, instead of, say, a 256-bit addressing space, is that the larger the addressing space, the larger the need for the IP header. In the early days of computing, bandwidth was exceptionally valuable; besides, a 32-bit addressing space would allow for nearly 4.3 billion addresses or devices connected to the Internet. That's enough, right? Well, as it turns out, the Internet exploded in popularity and so did the global population. This has led to what's known as IPv4 exhaustion. We'll cover this in more detail during the "NAT – Network Address Translation" section of this chapter.

IPv4 itself is a connectionless protocol and does not guarantee the reliable delivery of packets. Unreliability means that packets might never arrive at their destination or packets may arrive in the incorrect order or even arrive duplicated. These errors, including data integrity, are handled by the upper layer – the transport layer. Like TCP and UDP packets, or "segments" as the correct terminology in their respective layer, IP also has packets. These packets encapsulate their upper layer neighbor's segments for use in the network layer.

Much like TCP and UDP segments, IPv4 packets contain a header and its respective payload. In this case, the payload is a TCP or UDP segment.

The IPv4 packet itself is 24 bytes.

Let's take a look at how an IP packet looks like in Figure 2-5.

Anatomy of an IP Packet					
Version	Length	Service Type		Packet Length	
Identification				Flags	Fragment Offset
Time to Live		Protocol		Header Checksum	
Source IP Address					
Destination IP Address					
Options					Padding
Data/Payload					

Figure 2-5. *The anatomy of an IPv4 packet, with a header size of 24 bytes*

Now, unlike the TCP and UDP segments, IPv4 packets don't care about the payload contents. The purpose of IPv4 packets is to get the segment from the transport layer, then convert it into a packet for the network layer.

This IP packet has a few notable fields. The most important ones to be aware of are the following:

- **Source IP address** - The origin of the IP packet, which is the sender's IP address.

- **Destination IP address** - This is the destination IP address of the packet.

- **Total length** - The total length of the packet, with the minimum size being 20 bytes and the maximum size being 65,535 bytes. If the data is larger than 65,535 bytes, then the packet needs to be fragmented into multiple packets. The sender or a router generally does this. The receiving device does the reassembly of fragmented packets.

- **Identification** - This field allows for identifying groups of fragmented IP packets.

- **Protocol** - Defines the transport layer protocol within the payload. It is typically TCP or UDP; however, several other protocols exist.

- **Version** - The version of the IP packet; in IP version 4, this value is always 4.

IPv4 relies on IPv4 addressing. Let's discuss this in some more detail.

Addressing

In order for IP packets to know where they came from, and where they're going, each device connected to the network requires a unique IPv4 address. This IPv4 address is a 32-bit integer value, most often represented in dot-decimal notation. This dot-decimal structure consists of four octets of the address, expressed individually in decimal numbers separated by a dot or period.

These binary octets look something like this:

10010011.10011101.11010101.01110100

However, because they're represented individually in decimal numbers, those binary octets look more like the following to the user:

147.157.213.116

The preceding number is a typical representation of an IPv4 address. Since each piece of an IPv4 address is represented by an 8-bit octet, our minimum decimal value is 0, and the maximum value is 255.

This gives us roughly 4.3 billion unique IP addresses to identify devices on the global network or the Internet.

However, there are more than 4.3 billion devices that need to be connected to the Internet. So that's a problem. We'll cover how computer scientists created a workaround to this problem while the world very slowly transitions to IPv6, in the "NAT – Network Address Translation" section of this chapter.

ARP – Address Resolution Protocol

The Address Resolution Protocol is a communication protocol that allows for the discovery of data-link layer addresses, typically that of network layer addresses such as Ipv4. These addresses are generally in the form of MAC (Media Access Control) addresses. In IPv6, the neighbor discovery protocol (NDP) is used instead of ARP. ARP works on a request response structure, and ARP messages only communicate within their network boundaries. We'll discuss how ARP fits into the flow of data a little later on in the book, but for now, let's take a look at how ARP works (Figure 2-6).

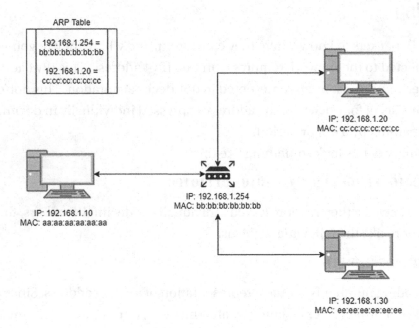

Figure 2-6. *We will use the example network in the figure to explain the Address Resolution Protocol*

Let's say you're on a device with the IP address of 192.168.1.10, and you need to send your player health to a player on the same network as you, with the IP address of 192.168.1.20. You know their IP address, but you don't know their MAC address, meaning your Ethernet card doesn't have a destination to send the data. In this case, your device will put together an ARP request with your IP address, your MAC address, and the IP address of the recipient whose MAC address you need to find. The Ethernet card will then send this ARP request out to the network.

The ARP request then arrives at your router. Your router then adds the IP address of your machine to its own ARP table. It then checks to see if its ARP table contains an entry for 192.168.1.20. In this example, we'll say that the router doesn't yet have an ARP table entry for 192.168.1.20. It duplicates the ARP request and rebroadcasts it out of each network port, an action known as "flooding."

Device 192.168.1.30 receives the ARP request and sees that the request is for a different device, adding the router to its ARP table and ignoring the request. Finally, 192.168.1.20 receives the ARP request. It adds the router to its ARP table and adds 192.168.1.10 to its ARP table. It then compiles an ARP response. Looking at its own ARP table, it can determine that the destination MAC address is cc:cc:cc:cc:cc:cc. The ARP response then travels to the router. The router receives the ARP response and passes it on to 192.168.1.10 while adding 192.168.1.20 to its own ARP table so future requests are easier to handle.

DNS – Domain Name System

So, what happens if you don't know the IP address of the destination or you want to migrate your game server to a new host, with a new IP address, without needing to deploy an update to your clients? That's where the domain name system comes in.

At its core, it's the system that allows you to type in "www.google.com" into your web browser and get to 172.217.170.78. The domain name system is essentially a glorified directory, with human-readable addresses that your device can cross-reference to get the corresponding IP address. It's worth noting that DNS uses multiple servers and is a decentralized service.

Another vital thing to note about DNS servers is that different users worldwide can receive different responses for the same DNS entries. If you were to type "ping www.google.com" into your command prompt, you'd likely receive a different IP address to the one previously mentioned. This ability for DNS to provide proximal responses gets employed by major Internet services, such as Google. This proximal response could allow you to configure a game server in America and Europe – tied to the same DNS address. However, there are other alternatives for game servers in an actual deployed environment, which we will discuss later in this book.

DNS Databases typically store the following information:

- **SOA** - Start of authority
- **A or AAAA** - IP addresses

- **MX** - SMTP mail exchangers

- **NS** - Name servers

- **PTR** - Pointers for reverse DNS lookups

- **CNAME** - Domain name aliases

Although DNS databases are generally not intended to be all-purpose databases, they have expanded to include the following occasionally:

- **DNSSEC** - Domain Name System Security Extensions

- **RP** - Responsible Person (RP)

- **RBL** - Real-Time Blackhole List (RBL)

The records that we're most interested in are the **A records**, as we can use these to point to our game servers or a matchmaking server.

A key takeaway here is that in multiplayer development, we can use DNS to redirect users without disrupting their service or without the need to deploy a patch for a backend change.

How a Headshot Travels Around the World

Packets, segments, ARP, protocols, and a whole bunch more – it can get overwhelming. So, let's recap what we've learned so far. Networking, and by extension, the Internet, relies on joint agreements known as standards. These standards allow vendors, researchers, and computer scientists to develop protocols. A protocol is a set of rules to be followed. This set of rules provides for the sustainable expansion of technology.

The primary networking protocol is known as the Internet Protocol Suite and defines five layers of abstraction that facilitate the replacement of older technologies with newer ones. These layers are known as the IP Model. The IP Model layers may only interact with the layer below and above it.

This separation of responsibility of the IP model layers means that if hardware advances faster than software, the software will not be affected or vice versa.

Let's recap these five layers:

- Layer 5, the application layer - This is where our game lies – our data, our players, and the logic that makes our game a game. We can't go up from the application layer, so instead, networked data needs to go to, or be received from, the layer beneath.

- Layer 4, the transport layer - Here, the *data* gets packed into *segments* or unpacked from segments into data for the application layer. Segments are neat little boxes that translate our data into the format needed by the layer below. Alternatively, the transport layer can unpack these segments and pass them up to the layer above.

- Layer 3, the network layer - This is where the segments get packed into packets. Packets are like neat little parcels, with their source and destination addresses labeled onto them and additional information required by the layer below. The network layer is responsible for packing layer four segments into packets or unpacking layer three packets into segments for the transport layer above.

- Layer 2, the data-link layer - This layer is responsible for taking layer three packets and placing them in frames. These frames are then ready to be split and sent through the layer below on their journey. Alternatively, these frames can be reconstructed back into packets and passed up along to layer three.

- Layer 1, the physical layer - This is where frames travel along their journey through a transport medium such as WiFi, Ethernet, or fiber.

When it comes to creating multiplayer games, we're generally only interested in the application and transport layers. The rest of the layers are not our problem or responsibility. But, knowing what these other layers do, their limitations and requirements will help you create multiplayer games that are scalable and push the boundaries of what's possible. It'll also help you debug and possibly avoid frustrating bugs.

So, what happens when you're playing a first-person shooter and the player on the opposing team hits you with a 360 no-scope headshot? Let's break it down.

Anatomy of a Headshot – Example Story

So, you're playing your favorite first-person shooter. You're racking up kills and carrying your team, team blue. You're doing great until you open the door in front of you, and you see that dreaded screen – you died. A player by the name of BilboSwaggins was responsible for your death.

Let's pause right here and dissect the scene from a networking perspective. You and BilboSwaggins have the same game, with the same scene loaded – the environment that you can both move around in. Different game engines use different terminologies to describe a scene or a map. For the sake of this book, we will be referring to the object that stores the actively loaded environment by its Unity terminology, a scene.

Generally, we don't synchronize the map over the network – objects such as the map are nonnetworked objects, which we update between game patches. However, we can network some aspects within the environment, like the door that you opened. Is the door open or closed? How wide should the door open? Where is the hitbox of the door?

We synchronize dynamic elements over the network to ensure that the state of the scene is the same for all players. The moment we replicate an object over the network, we call it a network entity. Network entities exist on the server, and clients subscribe to the network identity, creating an illusionary copy of the object. This copy is generally a read-only copy, with the server being the source of authority. When you open the door in most networking architectures, you're not the one opening the door. What happens is that you send a request to the server to open the door. We'll discuss authority and different types of game network architectures later in this book, but the server controls all game world elements in this example.

In theory, you could replicate all game objects in the scene, but the more elements you replicate, the more network entities exist. Unnecessarily replicating game objects can become very network-intensive very quickly, especially as more and more players connect to your server.

Let's say that you decide to replicate all of the game objects in your scene. Let's say 1000 of those game objects become network entities in your scene. You have ten players connected. Suddenly, 1000 entities need to be replicated to 10 clients. That's 10000 replications. Or, you could have 100 network entities in your scene, with 100 players connected. There, you have 10000 replications again, but 10 times the player count. Now, there are many other factors to consider, and it's not quite that simple, but it gets my point across. We generally only replicate game objects that are important to the multiplayer experience to reduce our network load as much as possible. Reducing our network load becomes even more noticeable when you're running hundreds of servers. Suddenly, the optimizations you've made are saving your company hundreds, thousands, or even millions of dollars in hosting.

Let's get back to our example. You decide to open the door to exit the building. You press the interact key while facing the door. The key that you pressed fires off a network command. We'll get into these in more detail later, but in short, a command is a request from a client asking the server to execute a method that it has authority over. The server sees that you'd like to interact. It then looks at your position and fires a ray cast from your player object forward, hitting the door. By doing this, the server is validating that you are in front of the door. It then executes the interaction logic on the door, opening the door.

The server then replicates the door's state back to all players, including yourself and your new arch-nemesis – BilboSwaggins. Sadly, BilboSwaggins lives closer to the server and receives the door state message from the server before you do. He turns to you and shoots you.

In the earlier example, the door's state is the data of the application layer. The application layer then passes the data to the transport layer – getting it ready to be sent on its long journey across the ocean.

The Importance of Keeping Your Packets Small

Replicating game objects and information over the network requires sending and receiving packets of information from your game clients. Keeping your packets small is paramount to the player experience, server costs, and overall scalability of your product.

The size of your data is probably tiny at a glance – a few bytes here, a few bytes there. Not caring about packet size can quickly grow out of hand. This unsustainable packet growth becomes noticeable when you start scaling up your product to potentially millions of players, let alone the players in your current game session.

The three major optimizations to keep in mind are the following:

- Only send necessary data.

- Only send data when it's needed.

- Data types matter.

Let's take an example. You'd like to replicate the state of the door in the example that we discussed in "How a Headshot Travels Around the World." You could have a door class with the following variables:

bool isOpen = true;

double openAmount = 0.8;

string animationName = "Swing";

In this example, we can see a poor implementation of a door that doesn't care about packet size. Sure, from the given data, we know that the door is mostly open. However, let's stop for a moment to consider the following.

You are sharing three properties of this class over the network. A bool costs 4 bytes of data, our double costs 8 bytes of data, and our animation name costs 10 bytes of data. That's 22 bytes of data per packet on this door, which doesn't seem like a lot. For some reason, your door's data is being sent at the server tick rate regardless of change. So every second, you're updating the state of your door 60 times to all of your players. The example is a horrible implementation of a door because it now costs you 1.289KB/s per player, per door, but you also need to receive the data from your players. Taking transmit and receive data, we're now looking at 2.578KB/s per player per door.

Your map has 20 doors, with 100 players in each session. That's 5MB/s per session on doors alone.

What if you have 100,000 players active across all of your servers, so, 1000 sessions? That's 4.91GB/s or 39.28Gbps of bandwidth across all of your servers that a poorly implemented door is costing you. What's that in terms of revenue?

Well, an estimated pricing of $0.15 per GB for the sake of this example puts us at $0.73 per second for this horrible implementation of a door. Still doesn't sound like a lot? That's ~$1,909,008 per month on the bandwidth alone of a mundane door.

Firstly, your game would never reach a player base of 100,000 active players with such horrible code and networking implementation – but I'm trying to get my point across. Twenty-two bytes is not a lot of data until it costs you nearly $2 million a month.

That brings me to my first optimization point.

Only Send Necessary Data

We can remove two of those properties from the network entirely and retain the same functionality. Let's get rid of *isOpen* and *animationName* from the network. We can locally calculate those variables purely by knowing how far open the door is. So let's keep *openAmount* for this example.

Now we're down to 8 bytes per packet. We know if the door is open if the open amount exceeds a threshold so that data doesn't need to go over the network. We also only have one animation on the door, which we can store in our local code.

Great, it's starting to look a little better – 8 bytes per door. Let's run it through the same logic recently given. We're now at ~$695,228 per month for the poorly implemented door. Still terrible, but we've more than halved our data cost by simply working more intelligently.

Let's explore the next optimization point.

Only Send Data When It's Needed

You don't need to send data every frame, and you generally shouldn't! In the previous examples, we're sending data at the server's tick rate. The tick rate is essentially the server's network frames per second.

But here's the thing, we don't need to know about a door's data if it hasn't changed. Thankfully, the networking gods have thought of this. When we discuss Mirror later in this book, we'll learn about an attribute called SyncVar. In short, we can mark a property as a SyncVar, allowing the value to replicate over the network but only when the value changes or a new client connects.

Great, it means that instead of replicating our door 60 times a second, we can reduce this to only replicate when the door is moving. Let's say on average, our door only needs to replicate once every 2 seconds. The majority of the time, a door won't be moving. So we're now down to 8 bytes per packet every 2 seconds. That's 4 bytes per second, per door, per player.

Let's run the same math as before. We're now at ~$5,793 per month to implement our door instead of over $1 million. That's a *lot* better, but there's still something that we've overlooked.

Data Types Matter

Data types are not equal. Each has its uses and corresponding size, as well as limitations. These sizes or memory footprints also affect the size of the data sent over the network. Generally speaking, there is a 1:1 relation between the memory footprint and the size of the data without compression. However, we need to remember what we learned earlier in this book. The data goes into a segment, which goes into a packet. Those segment and packet headers also have an associated cost.

In the example that we're currently discussing, we've excluded counting the headers' size to focus on optimization at an application level. So let's focus back on the data types by looking at Figure 2-7.

Data Size Comparison

Data Type	Range	Network Size*	Description
byte	0 to 255	1	Nonarithmetic, number in a given range. Always non-negative. Could be used in some niche situations, internally any arithmetic promotes a byte to an int. Generally use int instead.
sbyte	0 to 255	1	Nonarithmetic, number in a given range. Always non-negative. Could be used in some niche situations, internally any arithmetic promotes a byte to an int. Generally use int instead.
short	-32,768 to 32,767	2	Nonarithmetic, number in a given range. Could be used in some niche situations, internally any arithmetic promotes a short to an int. Generally use int instead.
ushort	0 to 65,535	2	Nonarithmetic, number in a given range. Always non-negative. Could be used in some niche situations, internally any arithmetic promotes a ushort to an int. Generally use int instead.
int	-2147483648 to 2147483647	4	Numbers not exceeding ~9 Billion, negative or positive. Good for counting things like score, player gold coins, etc.
uint	0 to 4,294,967,295	4	Number in a given range. Always non-negative. Useful for things like player id.
long	-9,223,372,036,854,775,808 to 9,223,372,036,854,775,807	8	Number in a given range. Useful for when very large numbers with negatives are needed. Great for cookie-clicker style games.
ulong	0 to 18,446,744,073,709,551,615	8	Number in a given range. Always non-negative. Useful for maximizing the length of a number when the number never needs to be negative.
float	-3.402823e38 to 3.402823e38	4	Number in a given range, can contain decimals. Useful for numbers that need decimal support, and minor loss of fractions are not critical. Things like player health, currency, and movement speed.
double	-1.79769313486232e308 to 1.79769313486232e308	8	Number in a given range, can contain decimals. Useful for when you need a large decimal value where accuracy is important.
decimal	(+ or -)1.0 x 10e-28 to 7.9 x 10e28	16	Number in a given range, can contain decimals. When you need an extremely large decimal value and accuracy is important.
char	Any valid character	2	Any valid single character. Generally not used alone, but could be used for things like delimeters in string formatting.
string	0 - 1073741791 chars	varying	Any valid characters not exceeding ~1 Billion characters. Mostly used for text, things like text chat, item names, descriptions, etc.
bool	True or False	4	Representation of either true or false. Useful for if-statements. Examples could be tracking what quests a player has completed.
Vector3	float, float, float	12	A three float struct, typically used to represent things like player positional co-ordinates.
Quaternion	float, float, float, float	16	A four float struct, typically used to represent rotation without the pitfalls of euler rotations.
Rect	float, float, float, float	16	A four float struct representing the corners of a rectangle.

Vector3Int	int, int, int	12	A three int struct. This could be used in niche scenarios where you need three ints representing a value.
URI	6 chars - 65,519 chars	varying	Uniform Resource Indicator, represented as an object. Typically constructed from a string.
Network Identity	uint	4	A component used to identify objects over the network, typically attached to any networked components.

Measured in bytes, excludes segment and packet overhead.

Figure 2-7.   *A chart representing the raw memory sizes for some of the commonly supported data types for Mirror*

Now generally, you don't need to worry too much about data types. Overoptimizing here can often waste time when we can optimize other things instead. However, it's essential to know that not all data types are equal.

Use the data type that is best suited for your needs. Let's compare our door's data types to that of Figure 2-7. In our door class, we're replicating **openAmount,** which will be a value of *0 - 1*, or perhaps in the future, we'll add the ability to break the door, in which case we could use *-1*. So, the whole range that **openAmount** will ever be is -1 to 1.

Our **openAmount** property is currently of the double data type. The double data type allows for a massive range with high fractional accuracy. This increased amount of data comes at a cost, however. So what other data type would let us have decimal numbers within our needed range? Look at Figure 2-7 and see if you can figure it out.

Looking at the chart, we need a data type that supports a number within our range and can support decimal fractions. We also don't need an extensive range. So an ideal data type to use here would be float.

A float will cost us 4 bytes of data instead of 8 bytes of the double type. That's half the required data, great!

Let's rerun the math at 4 bytes every 2 seconds, per door, per player, which brings us down to 2 bytes per second, per door, per player. That brings us down to ~$2,896 per month to implement doors in terms of bandwidth. Compare this to almost $2 million a month.

There are more ways to optimize this even further, like replicating a door only when the player presses the interact key. Instead of replicating a variable, we send a command to the server only when the player interacts with the door. We'll cover this in more detail later in the book.

Let's cover some more networking principles before going more in-depth into multiplayer.

Network Topologies

So we're starting to get an idea of how a device can send data to another device. If we have two devices connected, what happens when we want to add a third? How does the third device fit into this network relationship? That's where network topologies come in.

A network topology is the arrangement of devices on a network. Your home network is a great example of this. You likely have a router at home connected to the Internet. Connected to your router are all of your devices. This is an excellent example of a star topology.

If you're creating a game for consumers, then the most crucial network topology to learn and understand is the star topology. It's one of the most widely used network topologies. You can generally skip over the other topologies. However, if you're developing commercial networked applications within an old organization, you might encounter different network topologies. In this case, it would be wise to briefly touch on them, their purpose, and their pitfalls and understand that they exist and why the company used the topology in the first place.

It's also essential to mention that some of these other topologies get used by certain Internet service providers and other content providers. ISP infrastructure is out of the scope of this book, but it's good to keep in mind that just because we don't see a network topology, doesn't mean that it doesn't have a place.

Star Topology

The star topology is by far the most widely adopted network topology. We can largely attribute this extensive adoption to the ease of implementation, expandability, and ever-lowering cost of networking.

And why should you know about network topologies? You might decide to develop a local LAN game or enterprise application that runs on a local network.

So, where does the name come from, and what exactly is the star topology?

Devices connected in a star topology all connect to a central device. Generally, this device is a router. The connections, if mapped, form the shape of a star, hence the name.

Let's refer to Figure 2-8.

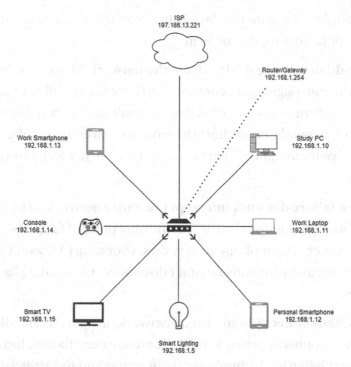

Figure 2-8. *The figure depicts a typical star network topology used in the majority of computer networks*

Looking at the figure, it starts to become clear where the topology gets its name. So how do does data travel in this topology?

Let's say you have an app on your personal smartphone to control your lighting. The app has a button that allows you to turn the lights on or off. Your personal smartphone has an IP address of 192.168.1.12. We learned earlier in this book that the IP address is an address used by the Internet Protocol version 4. When you press the button on your smartphone, the device packs your data into a segment, packed into a packet. The device then looks at its ARP tables and forwards the packet out to the router, located at 192.168.1.254.

From here, the router knows that the packet has the destination 192.168.1.5, the smart light. The router sends the packet to the smart light. The smart light's transport layer then unpacks the packet into a segment. The segment is then unpacked to its data and passed to the application layer, where the light determines that it needs to turn on.

So why do we use this topology?

There are a couple of contributing factors that lead to the mass adoption of the star topology. The major factors are the following:

- **Easily add or remove devices from the network** - This is likely one of the most significant contributing factors. The ability to add or remove devices easily means that we don't need to reconfigure our home networks every time a friend comes over to visit. We simply give them the WiFi password, and they're ready to browse the Internet.

- **A device failure does not interrupt the entire network** - The great thing about the star topology is that the only point of failure is the central router. If your phone battery dies, your smart TV won't lose connection, and your console won't disconnect while doing its hefty updates.

- **Well-suited for heavy load** - Home networks are good at handling massive amounts of network traffic. There are contributing factors, the largest being the technology in your router and the artificial limit that your router places on your Internet connection depending on the service package that you purchase.

- **Scalable** - A friend is coming over? Great! Ten friends coming over for a housewarming? No problem! Star topologies are highly scalable. Not enough signal in your bedroom? That's fine – place a repeater near the bedroom. A repeater is a device that acts as an extension of a router.

So, if star topologies are so great, then why aren't they the only topology around? Well, in the early days of computing, hardware was costly. With the mass adoption of information technology, IoT, and the cloud, hardware costs have dropped significantly.

Back in the day, it would cost companies insane amounts of money to set up large networks. So different network topologies were created to maximize the use of budgets, albeit inadvertently creating limitations for their networks.

So why learn them? As I mentioned earlier in the book, if you're developing for enterprise, there is an off possibility that you may encounter one of these other network topologies. It can be helpful to know what you're looking at so you can decide how to best proceed.

Bus Topology

This topology is an excellent example of a network that you're unlikely to find today. Bus networks are the remnants of an older era, and if you encounter this network topology during an enterprise deployment, you should highly consider upgrading the infrastructure.

These networks are all connected to a single cable, using t-connectors to tap into the mainline.

Let's take a look at Figure 2-9.

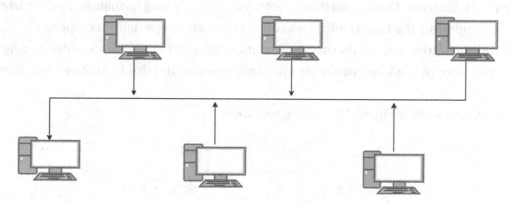

Figure 2-9. *The figure depicts a bus network topology. We seldom find this network topology today*

In the past, this network topology used significantly less cabling than the star topology and cost a lot less as there was no need for a router. However, deploying a bus network today would likely cost you significantly more than a star network. Along with the disadvantage of cost, there are the following disadvantages:

- **Bus networks are a pain to debug and diagnose** - One of the prominent reasons for this is that if a single t-connector fails, or if something goes wrong anywhere in the main cable, the network gets fractured in two. This fracturing results in a total network failure.

- **They're slow** - Typically, bus networks require the use of coaxial cables and t-connectors. These are usually limited to around 10–100mbps.

- **High packet loss** - Packets are often simply lost as a result of data collisions.

- **Non-scalable** - The bandwidth of a bus network gets shared among nodes.

Bottom line, avoid bus networks.

Ring Topology

Next up is ring topology. This network topology also gets its name from the shape of the network diagram. Devices on this network connect in a ring formation. In the early days of computing, the ring topology was quite successful, especially in corporate environments. However, as Ethernet became more adopted and costs went down, ring topologies were phased out. You're very unlikely to encounter this kind of network these days.

Let's take a look at Figure 2-10 of ring topology.

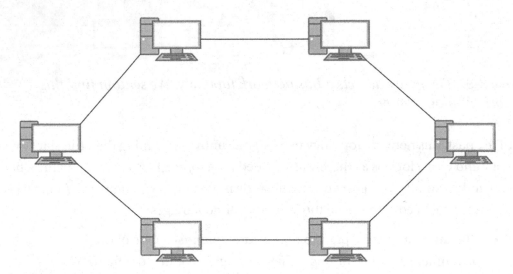

Figure 2-10. *The figure depicts a ring network topology*

Interestingly enough, ring topologies were so popular in the early days of computing that the IEEE recognized it as a standard, IEEE 802.5.

If you encounter this network in a commercial environment, you should deploy an updated network instead.

Mesh Topology

Next up, we have the mesh topology. Mesh topology is a network topology where all devices on the network connect directly with one another, forming a large mesh. One would think that you've never seen this kind of topology before. However, you'd be mistaken. We use mesh topologies for home automation, IoT, HVAC systems, electric smart meters, and more.

Let's take a look at Figure 2-11 to get a better understanding of mesh networks.

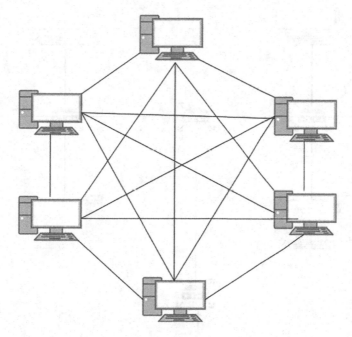

Figure 2-11. *The figure depicts a ring mesh topology where each device gets connected to every other device on the network*

It's important to note that in modern environments, devices do not need to mesh fully. Not needing a full mesh means that modern mesh networks get configured to mesh partially, connecting only to devices in the WiFi range.

Hybrid Topology

The hybrid network topology, or a hybrid network, as it's typically referred to, is simply a network topology that consists of more than one network topology on the same network. As such, it shares many of the advantages and disadvantages of the topologies that it uses.

Let's have a look at Figure 2-12 to get an idea of how hybrid networks look.

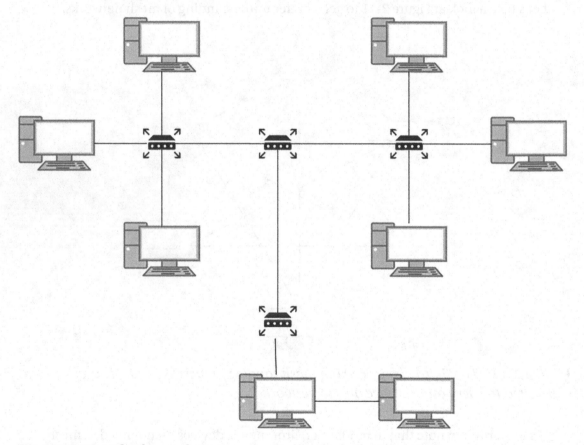

Figure 2-12. *The figure depicts an example of a hybrid topology*

We have a star network on the left connected via bus topology to another bus topology and another star topology on the right-hand side. Therefore, this example of a hybrid network consists of star and bus topologies. I'd like to emphasize that hybrid topologies don't need to exist from star and bus networks. There are many other variations of hybrid topologies.

Tree Topology

Tree networks are a form of hybrid topology, very similar to the example I just showed. Tree topologies consist of star topologies connected via bus topology. Where our hybrid topology example has an additional bus network, the tree topology is a bit different.

Let's take a look at Figure 2-13 to see how they look.

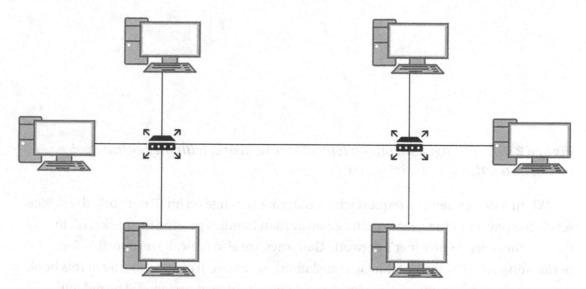

Figure 2-13. *The figure depicts a tree network topology. It consists of two star networks connected via bus topology*

Gateways

So, what happens when we need to connect two or more distinct networks in the case of the Internet? In networking, we have what's called a network gateway. This gateway is a device, and typically a router is your network's entry and exit point. Gateways are aware of local and outside networks. They are responsible for acting as an intermediary.

Looking at Figure 2-14, we can see where the gateway fits into a network.

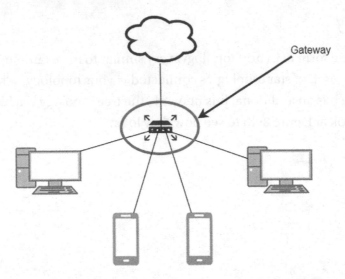

Figure 2-14. *The figure depicts a typical star network, with the central device acting as a gateway, circled in red*

When a device sends a request with a differing IP range on an IP network, the device sends the packet to the gateway. The gateway then handles passing the packet off to the Internet service provider's network. Gateways are also typically responsible for performing NAT (Network Address Translation), which we'll discuss shortly in this book.

Typically, on IP networks, devices have a default gateway assigned. The default gateway is either set manually or obtained from the DHCP (Dynamic Host Configuration Protocol) server. Let's discuss DHCP, one of the most used protocols that help networks remain scalable and user-friendly.

DHCP – Dynamic Host Configuration Protocol

If every device on an IP network needs a unique IP address, how do we ensure that new devices connecting to our local network each have a unique IP address? And how do we make local networks accessible for those who know nothing about networks or even computers?

You could go to every device on your local network, check their IP address, and then find an address that is not in use. You'd then have to assign the IP address to the device, set the default gateway, and hope that someone else doesn't choose a conflicting address. However, this isn't very practical, doesn't scale very well, and requires technical knowledge.

What if there was a way to ask the router what IP addresses are not in use and then assign that unused IP address to the device? Well, it turns out there is. It's called the dynamic host configuration protocol.

DHCP is a network discovery protocol that allows us to discover our network configuration to communicate on a network correctly. If you visit your friend's house, they may have a network with a completely different network configuration to yours, yet, when you go home, your mobile device connects to your home network and functions without issue.

Most modern routers have a built-in DHCP server. The DHCP server is the central authority on a network that manages the protocol and network configuration for its network section (Figure 2-15).

Static Route   Dynamic Route   **DHCP**

The DHCP server automatically allocates and manages IP addresses of devices on the LAN or WLAN. The DHCP server function works only in routing mode.

Note: Modifying the DHCP server parameters will cause the associated CPE to restart. In this case, you need to log in to the Web UI again. Changing the IP address and subnet mask of the gateway may disable certain functions, such as DMZ, port mapping, static routing, and dynamic routing. If any of them is disabled, reconfigure them.

DHCP

IP Address:	192. 168. 8 . 1	
Subnet mask:	255 . 255 . 255 . 0	
DHCP server:	ENABLE	
DHCP IP range:	2 to 254	192.168.8.2 to 192.168.8.254
DHCP lease time (s):	57600	3600 to 86400

IP and MAC Address Association   **+ Add**

Figure 2-15. *The image is from a router's DHCP server settings within its control panel*

Each router's configuration panel will be slightly different, and there may be more advanced options that are vendor-specific. However, for the most part, the options available to you will be the following:

- **The option of turning the DHCP server on or off** - This may be helpful if you have another authority on the network to manage DHCP addresses and do not want conflicting DHCP servers.

- **The option to change the IP address of the DHCP server** - In case you'd like to point clients to a different DHCP server.

- **The IP address pool** - The range of IP addresses that the DHCP server is allowed to allocate. It's important to note that the DHCP servers generally do not perform conflict detection, so it's best practice to assign a pool that manual IP address assignments will not use.

- **The lease time of the IP address** - How long an IP address gets reserved for a device before needing to be re-requested.

- **IP address and MAC address association preferences** - Allowing you to specify a MAC address and an IP address preference for DHCP allocation. The DHCP server will then give priority to assigning that IP address to the given MAC address.

So how does it work? DHCP employs a connectionless model using UDP that we learned about earlier in the book. DHCP uses two ports for this UDP model: port 67 for the server and port 68 for the client. More on ports a little later in the book.

DHCP works in four distinct phases:

- Server discovery

- IP lease offer

- IP lease request

- IP lease acknowledgment

Let's review these phases.

Server Discovery

When a device needs to obtain an IP address through DHCP, it first needs to know the DHCP server's IP address. The client device broadcasts a UDP packet to port 67 on the subnet, using the destination address 255.255.255.255, resulting in a limited broadcast on the subnet. The broadcasted UDP packet contains a DHCPDISCOVER message.

IP Lease Offer

When the DHCP server receives a DHCPDISCOVER request from a client, the DHCP server treats the request as an IP lease request. The IP request is then processed, and the DHCP server then reserves an IP address for the client. Once complete, the DHCP server sends a DHCPOFFER message to the client.

The DHCP Offer contains the following information:

- **Client ID** - Typically, the client device MAC address.

- **Proposed IP address** - The IP address proposed by the DHCP server.

- **The subnet mask** - The subnet mask that the client should use.

- **Lease duration** - The duration of the IP address lease.

- **DHCP server IP address** - The IP address of the DHCP server making the offer.

Once the DHCP server sends the offer to the client, it's up to the client to accept the request.

IP Lease Request

When the client receives an offer from the DHCP server, it will reply by broadcasting a DHCPREQUEST message to the server, requesting the offered IP address. A client can receive offers from multiple DHCP servers but can only accept a single offer. Before accepting an offer, a client can send an ARP message to the proposed address – if there is no response, it can take the offer.

Once the client accepts the offer from a DHCP server, other DHCP servers will revoke their offer and return the proposed IP addresses to their available IP pool.

IP Lease Acknowledgement

Once the DHCP server receives the DHCPREQUEST message from the client confirming acceptance of an IP lease offer, the DHCP configuration process enters its final phase, the IP lease acknowledgment phase. During the acknowledgment phase, the DHCP server sends a DHCPACK message to the client device. This DHCPACK message contains the IP address lease duration and any additional configuration options requested by the client.

The protocol expects the client to switch its configuration to the agreed-upon settings.

DHCP Release

The Dynamic Host Configuration Protocol does have an implementation for the releasing of IP addresses. A client can send a request to the DHCP server notifying the server that the device no longer wishes to use the provided IP address. If this happens, the DHCP will release the IP address back into the available pool, and the server expects the client to stop using the IP address. However, since it's not always possible to determine when a user will unplug or disconnect their device from the network, the protocol does not mandate sending a DHCPRELEASE message.

NAT – Network Address Translation

Let's talk IPv4 address exhaustion. We briefly covered this global crisis in the IPv4 section of this chapter, but if we've run out of unallocated IP address blocks, then how is the Internet still functioning?

Back in 1993, a paper titled *Extending the IP Internet Through Address Reuse* was written, and a year later, it was published as RFC 1663. This paper described an early version of NAT or Network Address Translation, a proposed solution to buy the Internet time to solve the coming IP exhaustion crisis.

The paper proposed that instead of every device being globally unique, every device could be unique within a smaller region. This concept would become what's today known as Network Address Translation.

Network Address Translation allows us to map IP address space onto another, modifying the IP packets while they are in transit through the network. The ability to remap network packet destinations and origins means that we can have local networks connected to a larger, global internetwork.

So how does it work? Typically, network address translators use a one-to-many translation, mapping multiple private IP addresses to a single public IP address. This is common in configurations such as your home network, even your office network. Multiple devices connect to a centralized gateway, typically a router, which performs the address translation, essentially representing your network on the Internet.

The public IP address of the network's gateway is typically assigned by the Internet service provider. When traffic passes through the translator, outgoing packets have their origin IP addresses dynamically modified by the translator. These modified packets have their origin IP address changed to the public IP address of the gateway.

This allows receivers of the packets to know where to actually reply to; if the native address translation was not performed, the receiver of a packet would see a local IP address such as 192.168.1.10 as the origin. Since that would not be a unique IP address, replying to that destination would fail.

Well, what happens if a public server uses 192.168.1.10 as their IP address? In short, they wouldn't. Thanks to the agreed-upon networking standards, specific network ranges have been explicitly reserved for use within a private network. Let's have a look at some of these reservations (Figure 2-16).

Address block	Address range	Number of addresses	Purpose	Description
0.0.0.0/8	0.0.0.0–0.255.255.255	16777216	Software	Current network, only valid for source addresses.
10.0.0.0/8	10.0.0.0–10.255.255.255	16777216	Private network	Used for local communications within a private network.
100.64.0.0/10	100.64.0.0–100.127.255.255	4194304	Private network	Shared address space for communications between a service provider and its subscribers when using a carrier-grade NAT.
127.0.0.0/8	127.0.0.0–127.255.255.255	16777216	Host	Used for loopback addresses to the local host.
169.254.0.0/16	169.254.0.0–169.254.255.255	65536	Subnet	Used for link-local addresses between two hosts on a single link when no IP address is otherwise specified, such as would have normally been retrieved from a DHCP server.
172.16.0.0/12	172.16.0.0–172.31.255.255	1048576	Private network	Used for local communications within a private network.
192.0.0.0/24	192.0.0.0–192.0.0.255	256	Private network	IETF Protocol Assignments.
192.0.2.0/24	192.0.2.0–192.0.2.255	256	Documentation	Assigned as TEST-NET-1, documentation and examples.
192.88.99.0/24	192.88.99.0–192.88.99.255	256	Internet	Reserved.
192.168.0.0/16	192.168.0.0–192.168.255.255	65536	Private network	Used for local communications within a private network.
198.18.0.0/15	198.18.0.0–198.19.255.255	131072	Private network	Used for benchmark testing of inter-network communications between two separate subnets.
198.51.100.0/24	198.51.100.0–198.51.100.255	256	Documentation	Assigned as TEST-NET-2, reserved for documentation and examples.
203.0.113.0/24	203.0.113.0–203.0.113.255	256	Documentation	Assigned as TEST-NET-3, reserved for documentation and examples.
224.0.0.0/4	224.0.0.0–239.255.255.255	268435456	Internet	In use for IP multicast.
240.0.0.0/4	240.0.0.0–255.255.255.254	268435455	Internet	Reserved for future use.
255.255.255.255/32	255.255.255.255	1	Subnet	Reserved for the "limited broadcast" destination address.

Figure 2-16. *The figure showcases the reserved IP addresses and what they're reserved for*

So, based on the agreed-upon standards, we can determine what IP addresses are local; private IP addresses which will not be unique within the global Internet, or even accessible; and the public IP addresses that are.

When traffic passes through the Network Address Translator, the translator tracks information about the connection, adding it to a table to assist with replies. Packets passing from the public Internet, through the Network Address Translator to the client device typically have their destination addresses modified, instead of their origin addresses.

The vast majority of Internet traffic uses TCP and UDP; for these, a port number is also required. NAT has been extended to support Port Address Translation (PAT). PAT facilitates the translation of the port numbers within the native address translation process. NAT and PAT, or NAPT (Network and Port Address Translation), allows communication through a router but only when a connection originates from within the local network since it's the initial originating message that establishes the required information for the NAPT translation table. The translation table is how a NAPT device tracks active connections.

This means that a game client on the local network can connect to an external game server hosted on a public IP address – but a device on the public Internet cannot connect to a game server hosted on our local private network. This applies to other content too, such as websites, FTP servers, and more.

So, NAT, or NAPT, helps us with two things. It helps alleviate the global IPv4 address exhaustion crisis, and it allows devices on private networks to connect to publicly hosted content, in our case – game servers.

But what happens if we'd like our customers to be able to host a game session on their local network and have additional clients connect through the Internet? If NAPT only works for outgoing connections, then how do we handle incoming connections? The answer lies in an extension of NAT, called port forwarding.

Port Forwarding

Port forwarding, also known as Port Mapping, is an extension of the Network Address Translator. It allows us to redirect a communication request from a given address and port combination to another. Typically, port forwarding is used to make devices on a private network available to the public Internet. We discussed NAPT and learned that it only works for outgoing connections; port forwarding is an extension of NAPT that allows us to have incoming connections to our local private network by remapping destination addresses and port numbers to that of a device within the local network.

Port forwarding typically requires a network administrator to configure the port forwarding on the network gateway. This can be done on most routers. The configuration panel usually looks something like Figure 2-17; however, it will vary between devices.

Application	Port from	Protocol	IP Address	Port to	Enable
ync-server1	5190	TCP ⬍	192.168.1.20	5190	☑
ync-server2	5191	TCP ⬍	192.168.1.30	5190	☑
ync-server3	5192	TCP ⬍	192.168.1.40	5190	☑

Figure 2-17. *The figure shows an example of a router's configuration page for the port forwarding options*

It's important to mention that not all routers support port forwarding, especially in the case of ISP-provided routers with custom configurations. Some ISP networks do not support port forwarding. This is important to note when debugging or planning a software deployment.

So I've mentioned ports several times in the book already, but what exactly are they, and what do they do?

Ports

Ports are a type of communication identifier that uses a 16-bit unsigned number, with a range between 0 and 65353. Let's assume you're running a game server for your new game. You have a friend on the same network as you who attempts to join your game server. They enter your device's IP address and attempt to connect. The packet reaches your device, but from there, it has no idea what it needs to do, where it needs to go, or why it's there. The packet itself is only a container for data, so it's up to the operating system to determine what application that packet needs to go to.

That's where packets come in. Instead of using the name of the application – which could also compromise security by allowing third parties to know what applications you have running – we use what's called a port.

When the operating system sees a packet destined for a specific port, it knows what application is currently running on that port, and it can forward the packet to the given application, knowing that the application will know what to do with the given port.

Port numbers are always associated with an IP address and typically represented alongside the IPv4 address as follows:

192.168.10.1:**4000**

In the previous example, we know that the IP address is 192.168.10.1, with a port number of 4000. It's important to note that for TCP, only a single process may bind to a specific IP and port combination. For programs communicating using TCP, if two applications bind to the same IP address and port, there will be conflicts, known as Port Conflicts, which will result in undesired effects.

So if we're using TCP, how do we know what port number to host our game on? How do we know that the port number will not conflict with any other running software our customers might be using? 65353 ports are not a lot of ports.

The answer is working together with other developers; there are several standards in place when it comes to choosing a port number. These standards are put in place by the Internet Assigned Numbers Authority (IANA).

The full list of registered ports can be found on the IANA website, **http://iana.org**, under the Service Name and Transport Protocol Port Number Registry.

Ports are split into three categories.

Well-known Ports (0-1023)

These ports are a no-go when creating your own custom applications. They're some of the most highly used ports and are typically reserved for core systems. Here are some of the most well-known ports as an example (Figure 2-18).

Port Number	Purpose
20	File Transfer Protocol (FTP) Data Transfer
21	File Transfer Protocol (FTP) Command Control
22	Secure Shell (SSH) Secure Login
23	Telnet remote login service, unencrypted text messages
25	Simple Mail Transfer Protocol (SMTP) E-mail routing
53	Domain Name System (DNS) service
67, 68	Dynamic Host Configuration Protocol (DHCP)
80	Hypertext Transfer Protocol (HTTP) used in the World Wide Web
110	Post Office Protocol (POP3)
119	Network News Transfer Protocol (NNTP)
123	Network Time Protocol (NTP)
143	Internet Message Access Protocol (IMAP) Management of digital mail
161	Simple Network Management Protocol (SNMP)
194	Internet Relay Chat (IRC)
443	HTTP Secure (HTTPS) HTTP over TLS/SSL

Figure 2-18. *The figure shows an example of a router's configuration page for the port forwarding options*

Typically, when you deploy your networked application, you'll be running on a port outside of the well-known port range. In fact, many operating systems actually require special permissions to allow an application to bind to a well-known port to ensure the stability of an IP network.

Registered Ports (1024-49151)

Once you're over 1023 ports, you enter the registered port range. This port range is reserved for applications by the Internet Assigned Numbers Authority. When deploying a large-scale application within this port range, be sure to do your research on what ports are currently officially (and unofficially) registered to what applications.

Here are a few examples of registered ports within this range (Figure 2-19).

Port	TCP	UDP	Description
1024	Reserved	Reserved	Reserved
	Reserved		Reserved
1027		Yes	Native IPv6 behind IPv4-to-IPv4 NAT Customer Premises Equipment
1028			Reserved
1029	Unofficial		Microsoft DCOM services
1058	Yes	Yes	nim, IBM AIX Network Installation Manager (NIM)
1059	Yes	Yes	nimreg, IBM AIX Network Installation Manager (NIM)
1080	Yes	Yes	SOCKS proxy
1085	Yes	Yes	WebObjects
1098	Yes	Yes	rmiactivation, Java remote method invocation (RMI) activation
1099	Yes	Assigned	rmiregistry, Java remote method invocation (RMI) registry
			Reserved
1109	Unofficial		Kerberos Post Office Protocol (KPOP)[citation needed]
1113	Assigned	Yes	Licklider Transmission Protocol (LTP) delay tolerant networking protocol
1119	Yes	Yes	Battle.net chat/game protocol, used by Blizzard's games
1167	Yes	Yes	Cisco IP SLA (Service Assurance Agent)
1194	Yes	Yes	OpenVPN
1198	Yes	Yes	The cajo project Free dynamic transparent distributed computing in Java
1214	Yes	Yes	Kazaa
1220	Yes	Assigned	QuickTime Streaming Server administration
	Yes	Yes	Infoseek search agent
1234		Unofficial	VLC media player default port for UDP/RTP stream
1241	Unofficial	Unofficial	Nessus Security Scanner
1270	Yes	Yes	Microsoft System Center Operations Manager (SCOM)
1293	Yes	Yes	Internet Protocol Security (IPSec)

Figure 2-19. *The figure shows several ports within the registered ports range designated by IANA*

Be sure to check the IANA registry before deploying your game or multiplayer software.

The next set of ports are known as ephemeral ports.

Ephemeral Ports (49152-65353)

The ephemeral port range is designated by IANA for use by dynamic application or private applications and cannot be registered with IANA. These ports are great for testing applications or services. It might be unwise to deploy a production game or application due to the lack of registrations within this port range.

Security

Let's talk security. We won't go into too much detail here since there are several books on the topic and the field itself changes almost daily. However, there are some core security systems and principles to understand when working with networking. Understanding these systems and principles will make debugging your networked application or game significantly easier.

The Firewall

The firewall is a network security system designed to filter network traffic and prevent unwanted connections. We'll be discussing host-based firewalls. These are systems deployed on the host itself and can control network traffic or other system resources.

Generally, host-based firewalls are a part of the operating system, but there are also custom applications that can take the role of the firewall. It's worth noting that not all firewalls are host-based; you do in fact get specialized firewall hardware designed to do the same thing.

Firewalls operate by monitoring and blocking communications based on pre-configured policies, generally put in place by the operating system or system administrator. These host-based firewalls or application firewalls are capable of running at a high level, which in turn allows them to make decisions on what packets to let through based on more than just source/destination IP addresses and ports.

During this book, we'll be working with two main firewalls – the Windows Firewall and AWS Security Groups.

If you're hosting an application on a windows server, you'll need to configure a firewall policy to allow incoming connections to your application on the port that you've decided to bind your application server to.

You can access the Windows Firewall by typing "Windows Defender Firewall with Advanced Security" into the windows search bar or by typing "wf.msc" into a command prompt (Figure 2-20).

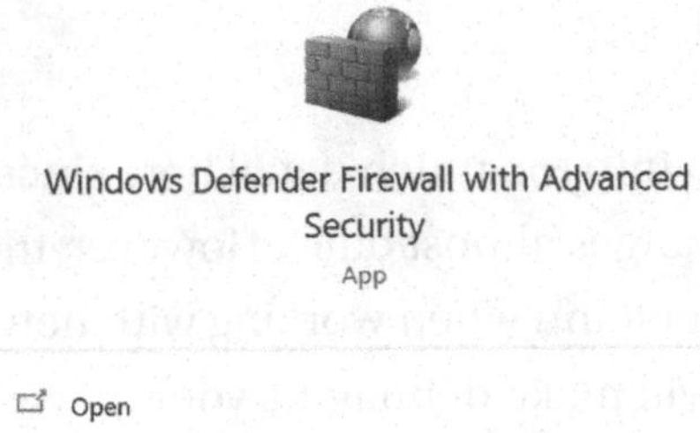

Windows Defender Firewall with Advanced
Security
App

⊡ Open

Figure 2-20. *The icon depicts a Windows Defender Firewall with advanced*
security

See the chapter exercises on how to open the Windows Firewall to a given
application or port.

Kinds of Attacks and How to Mitigate Them

Let's say that you're hosting a new multiplayer game and you somehow upset an
individual or group of players that now want to have revenge. It will experience nefarious
actors who wish to see the world and the game and burn throughout a game's life cycle.
These actors could be doing it out of spite from a developer action, out of spite of other
players or even just "for the lulz."

These actors are likely to employ a form of attack to affect the game and its
community negatively. It's important to know what kind of attacks you could expect
when hosting a multiplayer game, and while this list only covers a few of them, it should
form a solid foundation for researching other forms of attacks. I'll also be covering
attacks that are more focused on games, game servers, and their communities.

DDOS – Distributed Denial of Service Attacks

A typical network attack vector is a distributed denial-of-service attack. This kind of
attack works by overwhelming server resources or infrastructure with false requests from
hundreds, thousands, even millions of devices.

Typically, a DDOS attack is controlled by an attacker who has command of a botnet.
A botnet is a network of compromised, infected devices that nefarious actors can control
remotely. A DDOS attack is made practical because of the sheer number of attacking
devices. This large scale makes it extremely difficult to ignore requests from these
malicious devices since they may be making perfectly valid requests, just abusively.

The DDOS attack results in a denial of service to your non-malicious users by clogging up the server's resources or debilitating the hosted server's infrastructure. DDOS attacks are one of the most common attack vectors due to their ease of use. A malicious actor can pay someone in control of a botnet in order to use the network for their nefarious purposes.

There are three main kinds of DDOS attacks:

- **Application-layer DDOS attack** - This is where an attacker will flood the server with requests, in an attempt to have the server clog up by responding to valid requests.

- **Protocol attack** - These attacks are also known as state-exhaustion attacks, which attempt to cause a service disruption by overwhelming system resources by abusing the firewall or load balancers.

- **Volume attack** - Possibly the most common attack due to the simplicity behind it, this is where an attacker attempts to simply congest the bandwidth of a server by using a botnet or some form of amplification in order to create a massive volume of traffic.

So how do you prevent or mitigate a DDOS attack?

The main issue with DDOS attacks is the complexity involved with differentiating between normal, non-malicious requests and those of nefarious actors. This makes it challenging to differentiate between attacker and customer. Matters are further complicated when an attacker uses a multi-vector attack; this is when a DDOS attack uses more than one form of attack.

One method of countering a DDOS attack is called a blackhole route, where overwhelming traffic is routed to a null route, also known as a blackhole. In this scenario, both malicious and non-malicious traffic are dropped. It's not an ideal solution as this, in a large part, gives an attacker what they want, making your network inaccessible.

Rate limiting is another aid. Rate limiting is where you limit the number of requests a device can make within a given timeframe. Rate limiting is generally not enough to prevent a DDOS attack but can help with blocking malicious traffic.

Using a provider such as Cloudflare is another excellent option. Cloudflare uses an anycast distributed network, which allows you to spread the attack to the point where it becomes manageable. A DDOS attack would need to exceed ~67Tbps to cripple a Cloudflare network.

You could run your matchmaking services through Cloudflare to mask your actual server IP addresses and give out IP addresses dynamically as your hosting provider spools up new servers.

Hacking

Never trust your players. Your players will try to cheat at any available opportunity. In single-player games, this is not as much of an issue since the player only ruins the experience for themselves. However, in multiplayer, cheaters can be the sole reason for the death of a game.

Cheaters or hackers are detrimental to any gaming community, and you should deal with them to the best of your ability. Typically, a group of individuals will release or sell a "hack" for your game. A hack is a nefarious application that has outsmarted your game and can exploit vulnerabilities in your game to provide a cheater with an unfair advantage over other players.

Common types of game hacks include the following:

- **Aimbot** - This form of hack is most prevalent in first-person shooter games. It allows the attacker to have assisted aim. The hack software detects where the enemy player is and aims at them, optionally shooting. Typically, an aimbot aims for the head of the opposing player and allows the hacker to kill other players without much effort quickly.

- **Mobility-related hacks** - Another form of attack that many networked game architectures are vulnerable to is mobility-related hacks. This form of hack allows an attacker to modify variables of their player, adjusting speed, jump height, flying, or even walking through walls.

- **Extrasensory perception** - This attack is also known as ESP. It allows the attacker to have detailed information about other players, such as seeing them through walls, what kind of equipment they have, or how much health they have left.

The best way to deal with hackers is to choose a game architecture that is resistant to hackers. Any architecture that gives players any control over their player character will be highly susceptible to hacks. We'll discuss different game server architectures later in the book.

There are other ways to reduce the impact of cheaters and hackers. One of the main routes followed by companies releasing multiplayer games is the use of an anti-cheat. As the name implies, an anti-cheat prevents cheating or, at the very least, detects it.

Anti-cheats is a service provided to companies by the developers of these anti-cheat tools. The most notable ones are the following:

- **Easy Anti-Cheat** - A premium anti-cheat solution provided as a service. Easy Anti-Cheat protects some of the top competitive games globally, such as Apex Legends, Fortnite, Rust, and more.

- **Valve Anti-Cheat (VAC)** - Valve Anti-Cheat is an anti-cheat software developed by Valve. The Steamworks library provides various anti-cheat features and allows you to issue VAC bans to malicious players.

- **Anti-Cheat Toolkit** - Anti-Cheat Toolkit is a powerful anti-cheat and obfuscation tool available on the Unity Asset Store. This toolkit makes it significantly more challenging for hackers actually to create hacks in the first place.

The bottom line here is to use a highly authoritative networking architecture for your game server and implement at least one form of anti-cheat.

Review Bombing

Review bombing is an infamous Internet phenomenon in which large groups of users leave negative reviews in an attempt to harm game sales. Review bombing typically happens when a developer seems unresponsive to a specific perceived issue by the community. It's different from regular negative reviews, as the users rarely actually review the game itself. Instead, review bombs directly attack a company and can even target other games released by the same company. Due to the increasing prevalence of review bombing, many online distribution platforms have added systems to detect such practices. These systems will mark a period where reviews are marked as irrelevant and will not affect the game producer's total review score. Regardless of these measures, though, review bombing is often a symptom of an underlying problem.

Transparency and good customer relations are vital for avoiding review bombs.

Networking Diagnostic

When you're developing games, it's crucial to be able to debug your game. We'll cover some specific tools that I've used for debugging, deployment, and diagnostics.

Tools of the Trade

Various networking and diagnostic tools exist, but it's often difficult to get lost and not know what to look for when you need to debug an issue. So I've listed several tools that have helped me personally when debugging and deploying multiplayer products. These will just be brief introductions to the tools to help you know what to look for during your search.

Wireshark

Wireshark is a potent and versatile tool (Figure 2-21). Using Wireshark to debug game networks is akin to lighting a candle with a blowtorch, but sometimes, it's windy, so a blowtorch just does the trick.

Download: www.wireshark.org/download.html
Platforms:

- Windows

- Mac

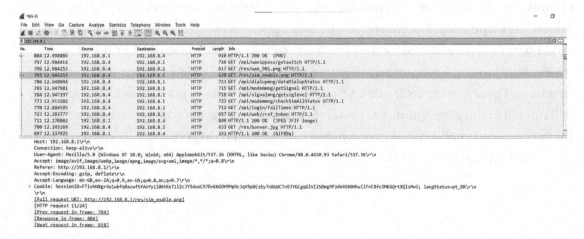

Figure 2-21. *A screenshot depicting the Wireshark interface currently capturing HTTP traffic on the WLAN adapter*

What Does It Do?

Wireshark is a powerful open-source packet analyzer, typically used for network troubleshooting, analysis, software development, and educational purposes.

When Do We Use It?

We use Wireshark when we want to break apart unencrypted packets sent and received from our game server. We can then ensure that the packets are in the correct format. Debugging packets at this level is helpful in a development environment when traffic is not encrypted or for testing that encryption is functioning as intended.

Nmap and Zenmap

Zenmap is the visual interface for Nmap, a robust network mapping and security tool (Figure 2-22).

Download: `https://nmap.org/zenmap/`

Platforms:

- Windows

- Linux

- Mac

Figure 2-22. *A screenshot depicting the Zenmap interface after running a simple, quick scan on my router*

What Does It Do?

Nmap is an extremely powerful security scanner. It supports various security tools, but the one we're most interested in is the ability to sniff for open ports. Nmap can be a helpful tool when troubleshooting connectivity to your game server.

When Do We Use It?

You should have Zenmap in your arsenal of debugging tools at all times. The tool is potent and worth learning. If you're having trouble connecting to a game server, consider running a port scan on the server to ensure that the port is open.

FileZilla

FileZilla is a free and open-source file transfer protocol application consisting of FileZilla Client and FileZilla Server (Figure 2-23). It allows us to deploy our files to the remote server used for hosting our test servers instead of copying them through the remote desktop protocol.

Download: `https://filezilla-project.org/download.php`

Platforms:

- Windows

- Linux

- Mac

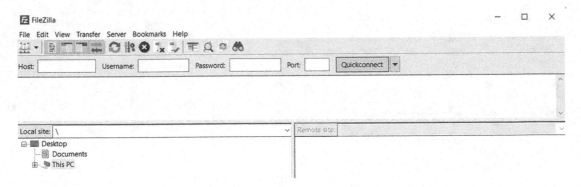

Figure 2-23. *A screenshot depicting the FileZilla interface awaiting connection to an FTP server*

What Does It Do?

FileZilla is a file transfer protocol (FTP) application that lets you quickly and easily transfer files between an FTP client (FileZilla Client) and an FTP server (FileZilla Server).

When Do We Use It?

We use FTP to upload files to remote servers since, in production, we will generally deploy our game servers automatically. We'll use this more during the development phase.

Windows Remote Desktop

Windows Remote Desktop is a remote desktop protocol client that allows us to connect to a remote Windows server and assume control of its desktop. Windows Remote Desktop (Figure 2-24) is powerful for managing Windows servers. It's worth noting that other RDP clients exist, but we'll be using the RDP client built into Windows for the sake of this book.

Download: Built into Windows, excluding Windows Home Edition.

Platforms:

- Windows

Figure 2-24. *A screenshot depicting the Windows Remote Desktop interface awaiting connection settings*

What Does It Do?

The Windows remote desktop client allows you to assume control over another windows machine, typically a windows server. The target device does not even need to be on the same network as you.

When Do We Use It?

We use Windows remote desktop typically when we're looking to configure our remote Windows servers.

Event Viewer

Event Viewer is a Windows tool that can be accessed by simply searching "event viewer" (Figure 2-25). The tool is essentially a unified log reader allowing you to view notable events that happened. The Event Viewer is a priceless tool for debugging application crashes that Unity just never caught.

Download: Built into Windows.

Platforms:

- Windows

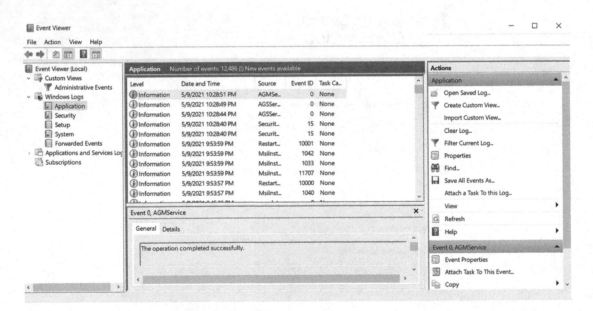

Figure 2-25. *A screenshot depicting the Event Viewer interface found on Windows*

What Does It Do?

The Event Viewer logs events that occur on the system, typically logging system services and application crashes. These crash logs can often contain information about what caused a crash that Unity may not detect in its logs.

When Do We Use It?

Use the Event Viewer if your unity logs and crash reports are failing to provide any helpful information.

Mirror Network Profiler

The Mirror Network Profiler is a powerful profiler extension for Unity that allows you to measure the performance of your networking code (Figure 2-26). Access to the tool requires you to become a GitHub supporter of Mirror, but this is well worth it.

Download: `https://mirror-networking.gitbook.io/docs/guides/network-profiler`

Platforms:

- Windows

- Mac

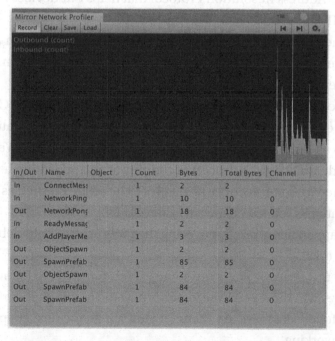

Figure 2-26. *A screenshot of the Mirror Network Profiler displaying network information*

What Does It Do?

The Mirror Network Profiler allows you to analyze your mirror networking code to determine performance and easily see where you can improve your code. It's an invaluable tool when developing multiplayer games with Unity using Mirror.

When Do We Use It?

We use this Unity extension while we're developing our multiplayer games and during optimization phases.

Summary

Well done on completing the chapter! In this chapter, we learned about computer networking, how conceptual models work, and the importance of standardization. We then learned about how TCP and UDP are data containers that format our application's data into segments compatible with the networking protocols in place with IP.

We learned how packets travel across the world using IPv4 and how each device on the public Internet has a unique address. We covered DNS and learned how www.google.com becomes an IP address.

We covered the Address Resolution Protocol that helps our devices know what MAC addresses map to IP addresses.

Then, we learned how packet size makes a massive difference when talking in scalable multiplayer systems, how we can optimize our network code, and how we can write scalable systems.

We then covered different network topologies and learned how DHCP servers work and what gateways are. We also learned how gateways perform native address translation to help alleviate the global IPv4 address exhaustion crisis. We also discussed how ports are an identifier for the processes running at an application level.

We then touched on some security principles to be aware of, such as the firewall and different kinds of attacks you may expect as a developer.

Finally, we wrapped up by briefly covering the tools used to help debug and troubleshoot networks.

That wraps up this chapter. There are some exercises for you to follow at the end of this chapter. They will show you how to perform some helpful networking tasks. I encourage you to follow them and try them for yourself. In the next chapter, we'll take a look at Mirror Networking.

Exercises

EXERCISE 1 – PINGING ANOTHER DEVICE

Ping is a simple yet powerful command-line utility that attempts to send packets of data to a destination device and listens for a response (Pong!). It is very easy to use and useful for seeing if you can connect to a given IP address.

Step 1 – Open the Windows Command Prompt by pressing Windows Key + R, then type *cmd* into the prompt box, and click *OK* (Figure 2-27).

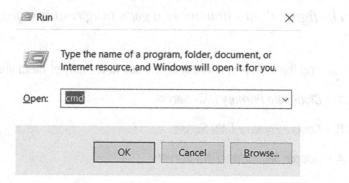

Figure 2-27. *The figure shows the Windows Run dialog*

Step 2 – You should now have the windows command prompt open. You can use the *PING* command using the following syntax: *ping [Address]*. Let's run the command *ping 127.0.0.1* by typing the command and pressing Enter. By sending a ping to the IP address 127.0.0.1, we are sending a packet to the "loopback adapter" of our device. This is a special address that refers to yourself. So we should get a reply unless something is horribly wrong. That reply should look something like in Figure 2-28.

```
Microsoft Windows [Version 10.0.19042.928]
(c) Microsoft Corporation. All rights reserved.

C:\Users\          >ping 127.0.0.1

Pinging 127.0.0.1 with 32 bytes of data:
Reply from 127.0.0.1: bytes=32 time<1ms TTL=128
Reply from 127.0.0.1: bytes=32 time<1ms TTL=128
Reply from 127.0.0.1: bytes=32 time<1ms TTL=128
Reply from 127.0.0.1: bytes=32 time<1ms TTL=128

Ping statistics for 127.0.0.1:
    Packets: Sent = 4, Received = 4, Lost = 0 (0% loss),
Approximate round trip times in milli-seconds:
    Minimum = 0ms, Maximum = 0ms, Average = 0ms
```

Figure 2-28. *The figure shows how we can get a ping response from our loopback adapter*

Done! Now try to ping the following addresses and see how many of them you can connect to:

- **1.1.1.1** – *Cloudflare Primary DNS Server*

- **8.8.8.8** – *Google Primary DNS Server*

- **4.4.4.4** – *Google Secondary DNS Server*

Bonus Objective

If you have a secondary Windows device available to you, try to find its IPv4 address by running the command ipconfig -all on the secondary device. Then, try to ping that address on your primary device.

EXERCISE 2 – PORT SNIFFING USING ZENMAP

Zenmap is a powerful security scanner, and it has many uses for network troubleshooting, penetration testing, and networked software development. We're going to use it to sniff for open ports on an IP address. This is very useful for determining if our game server port is configured correctly. Since we don't have a game server yet, we'll just be learning to use the tool to see what ports are available on a few devices. Eventually, you'll look to see if the specific port your game server is hosted on is accessible.

Step 1 – Download and install Nmap from the URL provided in the "Tools of the Trade" section of this chapter, under Nmap and Zenmap.

Step 2 – Zenmap is bundled with Nmap, meaning that by installing Nmap, you've installed Zenmap too. So, search for Zenmap in the Windows search bar, and launch it (Figure 2-29).

Nmap - Zenmap GUI

App

Figure 2-29. *The image shows the Nmap - Zenmap GUI app logo*

Step 3 – Enter the target, 127.0.0.1 (yourself) into the Target field, and change the profile to Quick Scan, before clicking the Scan button. Your Zenmap should look like Figure 2-30.

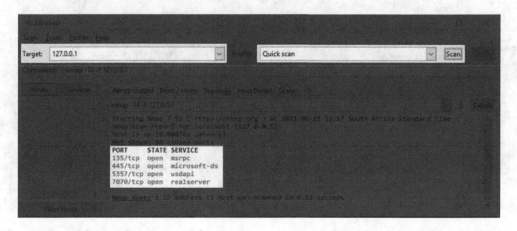

Figure 2-30. *The figure showcases how we can scan a target for open ports*

Nmap will now perform a quick scan on the loopback adapter. As with the previous exercise, we are targeting the "loopback adapter," which is assigned a special, reserved IP address of 127.0.0.1 and always points to yourself. When you have a hosted server available to use, you can point the scan at the server to determine if your game port is correctly accessible.

Done! You can now see a list of open TCP ports on the device. You can also adjust the can profile to scan for open UDP ports.

Next up, we'll learn about actually opening the ports on the Windows Firewall.

EXERCISE 3 – CONFIGURING THE WINDOWS FIREWALL

Before you have a game server, you'll need to know how to configure the Windows Firewall.

Without configuring the Windows Firewall, your users won't have a way of actually connecting to the game server. So, let's open the firewall to a port; it's recommended to do this in a sandbox environment. Alternatively, just remember to delete the record after completing the exercise. We wouldn't want to create any security risks.

Step 1 – Open Windows Firewall with Advanced Settings. You can do this by searching for it in the Windows search bar or pressing Windows Key + R, then typing in control firewall.cpl and pressing enter, then navigating to Advanced Settings on the left panel.

Step 2 – Now that you have Windows Firewall with Advanced Settings open, navigate to Inbound Rules, then select New Rule from the right-hand panel. See Figure 2-31.

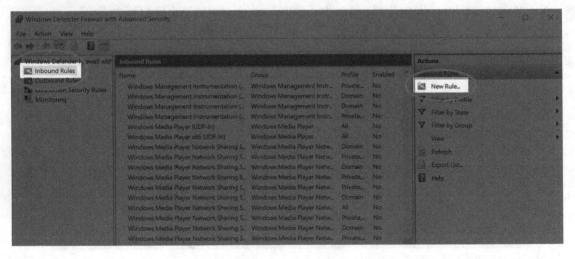

Figure 2-31. *The screenshot shows how we can add a new inbound firewall rule*

We're creating an Inbound Rule because we want incoming connections to be allowed to connect to us.

Step 3 – Select Port on this list of options that you'd like to create the rule for, then press Next (Figure 2-32).

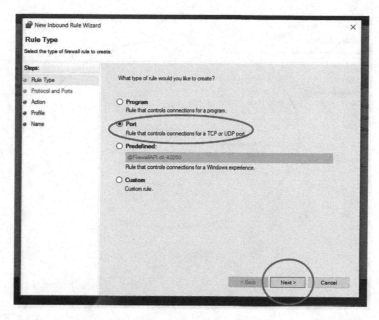

Figure 2-32. *The screenshot shows the steps required to configure the new firewall rule*

Step 4 – Select the type of port that you'd like to open. This will vary depending on your game server's transport layer. For the sake of the exercise, select TCP, and choose a number within the registered ports range discussed in the Ports section of the book. I'll be using port number 10101 (Figure 2-33).

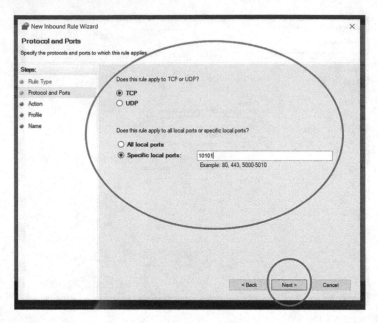

Figure 2-33. *The screenshot demonstrates how we can assign a port to the firewall rule*

Step 5 – Select Allow This Connection and click Next.

Step 6 – Ensure that Domain, Public, and Private are checked, and click Next.

Step 7 – Give your rule a descriptive Name and Description, and click Finish (Figure 2-34).

Figure 2-34. *The figure showcases the configured firewall rule*

Done! You can now find your Firewall Rule in the list of rules. If you'd like to delete the rule, select it, and press Delete on your keyboard, or choose the option on the right-side panel. I would suggest trying to use the port sniffing techniques learned in Exercise 2 in order to access the port.

EXERCISE 5 – USING THE WINDOWS EVENT VIEWER

The Windows Event Viewer is a useful utility for debugging when unity logs just don't cut it. This can be particularly useful if you experience a crash to desktop (CTD) while working on networked games. For the most part, it should never get to that point, but knowing what the Windows Event Viewer is, how to find it, and, most importantly, how to use it is key to successfully debugging particularly tricky bugs.

Step 1 – Search for the Windows Event Viewer in your Windows Search Bar; alternatively, press Windows Key + R in order to open the Run dialogue box. Type in eventvwr.msc and press Enter.

Step 2 – You should now have a window that looks like Figure 2-35.

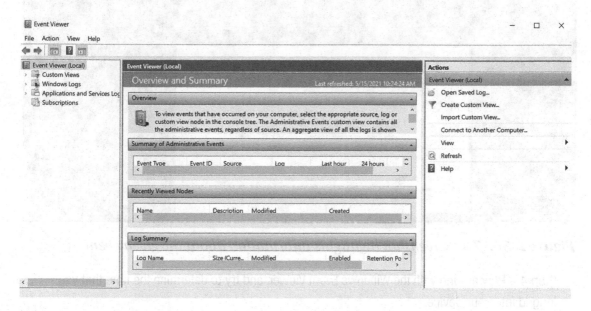

Figure 2-35. *The screenshot showcases the Windows Event Viewer app*

Step 3) Using the tree on the left, navigate to Windows Logs ➤ Application (Figure 2-36). In this view you'll see a detailed log of notable application events. This is broken down into three categories, Informational, Warning and Error, each denoted with a corresponding symbol.

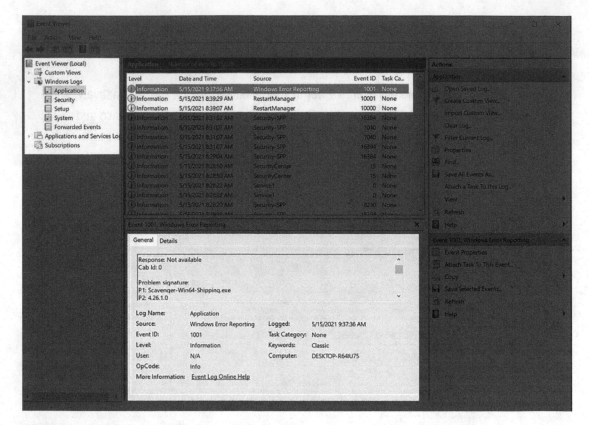

Figure 2-36. *The screenshot highlights information about the given event.*

Step 4 – Play around with the Windows Event Viewer, and try to determine the time that you logged into your device.

Tip: If you get stuck with Step 4, search for WinLogOnService.

Bonus: If you ever need to include very important information into the event log, you can use the EventLog.WriteEntry method provided by the System.Diagnostics namespace. But keep in mind that this should be used very sparingly; in general, you should always use the log file generated by Unity.

For more information on the EventLog.WriteEntry method, see the following URL:

https://docs.microsoft.com/en-us/dotnet/api/system.diagnostics.
eventlog.writeentry

CHAPTER 3

A Hall of Mirrors

Now that we understand networking basics, we can begin discussing multiplayer in
Unity in greater detail. We'll be using Mirror Networking to achieve scalable multiplayer
networking within Unity.

But, what exactly is Mirror Networking? Mirror Networking is a high-level networking
library released in October 2018. It was created to fix the neglected UNET and provide a
platform for other developers to expand upon it, submit improvements, and collaborate.

Mirror uses a Command-RPC networking structure, where each connection
requires authority over an object to modify it on the network. Mirror Networking is easy
to implement without sacrificing scalability. Mirror Networking is excellent for small
studios and large AAA studios aiming to create MMO scale networking.

The great thing about Mirror is that the client and the server are both a single project,
helping to increase productivity during development.

Architecture

As I mentioned briefly, Mirror uses a Command-RPC networking structure. A
Command-RPC architecture means that clients and servers communicate through
commands (Client-to-Server) and remote procedure calls (Server-to-Client). Commands
allow clients to execute a remote method on the server on an object they have authority
over. It's a way for the client to ask the server to perform a given command.

Inversely, RPCs allow the server to execute methods on the client remotely. This
back and forth between server and client forms the foundation of our networking,
allowing us to send a wide variety of supported data types and references over the
network. The Command-RPC architecture makes code a lot easier to follow than other
networking solutions.

© Dylan Engelbrecht 2022
D. Engelbrecht, *Building Multiplayer Games in Unity*, https://doi.org/10.1007/978-1-4842-7474-3_3

Additionally, we have things like SyncVars – synchronized variables. SyncVars are an easy and effective way of synchronizing variables and data across the network for existing and new clients joining a game.

Finally, we have the separation of Mirror Networking and the transport layer. Separating Mirror Networking and the transport layer is a potent level of abstraction that allows us to use different transport layer plugins to best suit our needs, as easy as swapping out a reference in the inspector. There are many transport layers to choose from, from those that come from Mirror Networking to the custom community-built transport layers.

These transport layers support TCP and UDP, so be sure to consider what protocol you want to use when making a decision. Let's take a look at the transport layers available to Mirror Networking.

Transport Layers

As TCP separates responsibilities into layers, so does Mirror Networking. While Mirror Networking itself is responsible for the high-level networking functionality, the Mirror Transport Layer is responsible for communicating at the transport layer level.

This abstraction is one of the reasons that Mirror is so powerful. It allows us to assign different transport layers based on our needs. The best part is that we're not even limited to a single transport layer! This customization and specialization allow us to get the most out of this networking solution, as each transport layer has various pros, cons, and supported platforms.

The most significant factors to consider when choosing a transport layer are the following:

- **TCP or UDP** - TCP is reliable out of the box but carries more network overhead. UDP is connectionless and unreliable in a network context. However, there are ways to get reliability out of UDP.

- **Reliable or unreliable** - Does the transport layer facilitate the reliability of a message that we send? In other words, do we have any guarantee that either the server or the client will receive messages sent?

- **Platform** - What platforms do the transport layers support?

- **Special considerations** - Does the transport layer have any specific requirements or special considerations that we need to make?

Comparing Transport Layers

Let's take a look at some of the transport layers available to us, and compare their strengths, weaknesses, and purposes. I'll briefly cover each of the major transports and then go into detail with my transports of choice (Figure 3-1).

		Y - Yes	U - Untested		N - No		K - Kind of				
Mirror Transport Layers											
Name	**Notes**	**Server**	**Client**	**Windows**	**Android**	**Linux**	**Mac**	**iOS**	**XBox**	**PS**
AsioTransport	Incredibly powerful server-side TCP and Websocket transport for dedicated servers.	Y	N	Y	U	Y	Y	U	U	U
LRM - LightReflectiveMirror	LRM is a self-hosted, open source, relay/NAT Punchthrough server. Supporting many different other transport layers. It requires the use of another Transport layer.	Y	Y	Y	Y	Y	Y	Y	U	U
EpicOnlineTransport	Epic is a free NAT punchthrough and relay server transport layer using Epic Games.	Y	Y	Y	U	Y	Y	U	U	U
Ignorance	High-performance reliable UDP transport layer using ENET.	Y	Y	Y	Y	Y	Y	Y	K	K
KCP	A C# KCP Implementation in Unity by Vis2k aimed at MMO scale networking.	Y	Y	Y	Y	Y	Y	Y	Y	Y
LiteNetLib	Lite reliable UDP library for .NET Framework 3.5, Mono, .NET Core 2.1, .NET Standard 2.0.	Y	Y	Y	Y	Y	Y	Y	U	U

Figure 3-1 Part 1. *The figure depicts the first six transport layers in the list*

Asio transport is an incredibly powerful server-site TCP and WebSocket transport that is intended for use with dedicated servers. The Asio transport is a serverside-only transport layer. It's one of the only transport layers available for Mirror that are exclusively intended for the server to use.

LRM is a self-hosted relay server that allows bypassing of troublesome NAT layers. It also provides basic NAT punch through, though it's important to note that NAT punching doesn't always work. LRM requires the use of another transport layer and simply adds additional functionality to the specified transport layer.

EpicOnlineTransport is a transport that leverages epic games' relay services. It requires an epic games developer account.

Ignorance is an extremely powerful reliable UDP transport layer that runs on ENET; overall, it's an incredible transport layer that you should definitely consider using.

KCP is one of my personal favorite transport layers and supports hundreds of players. It also has reduced latency at the cost of some extra bandwidth. We'll talk about this transport layer in more depth, shortly.

LiteNetLib is another great reliable UDP transport layer with wide platform support.

		Y - Yes	U - Untested	N - No	K - Kind of						
			Mirror Transport Layers								
Name	**Notes**	**Server**	**Client**	**Windows**	**Android**	**Linux**	**Mac**	**iOS**	**XBox**	**PS**
Monke	Monke is an encryption layer you can use for other transport layers. Requires the use of another Transport layer.	Y	Y	Y	Y	Y	Y	Y	Y	Y
Oculus P2P	This is a transport for Mirror that sends data via the Oculus Platform P2P service. Still in development and is not production ready at the time of writing.	Y	Y	Y	Y	U	U	U	U	U
FizzySteamworks	FizzySteamworks brings together Steam and Mirror. It supports both the old SteamNetworking and the new SteamSockets.	Y	Y	Y	N	N	N	N	N	N
FizzyFacepunch	This is an alternative version of FizzySteamworks that uses Facepunch instead of Steamworks.NET.	Y	Y	Y	N	N	N	N	N	N
Telepathy	Simple, message based, allocation free MMO Scale TCP networking in C#.	Y	Y	Y	Y	Y	Y	Y	Y	Y

Figure 3-1 Part 2. *Depicts the next five transport layers in the list*

Monke is an encryption layer intended to be used with another transport layer. Overall, it's something I'd recommend including in almost every project.

OculusP2P is a transport layer that leverages Oculus' relay servers; however, it's still in development, so I'd avoid using it in any production releases. It's still worth the mention, and you should keep an eye on it.

FizzySteamworks is a transport layer that leverages Steamworks to allow for the use of steam and Mirror.

FizzyFacepunch, much like FizzySteamworks, brings in the functionality of a third party, this time allowing you to use Facepunch instead of `http://steamworks.net`.

Telepathy is a tried and tested transport layer; we'll discuss this in more detail shortly.

		Y - Yes	U - Untested	N - No	K - Kind of						
		Mirror Transport Layers									
Name	Notes	Server	Client	Windows	Android	Linux	Mac	iOS	XBox	PS
Simple Web Transport	This Transport uses the websocket protocol. This allows this transport to be used in WebGL builds of unity.	Y	Y	Y	Y	Y	Y	Y	U	U
Mirror WebRTC	The purpose of this transport is to provide an alternate method of online connectivity that does not require port forwarding by the game host.	Y	Y	Y	U	U	U	U	U	U

Figure 3-1 Part 3. *Depicts the final two transport layers in the list*

SimpleWebTransport is your go-to when you need web apps to connect to your mirror network or vice versa. It's one of the few transport layers that support WebSockets.

Mirror WebRTC is a kind of decentralized relay service that extends the functionality of another transport.

Additional Transport Component Logic

In addition, transport layers can also act as an intermediary to other transport layers. They can provide additional logic and functionality, such as adding encryption or providing NAT punch-through. A great example of this is Monke's ability to provide encryption for your data passing through the transport layer.

This handover of transport layer data also opens up the possibility for other transport layer additions, such as the fallback transport component.

Fallback Transport Component

The fallback transport component is a great way to work around platform limitations. It allows us to switch to other transport layers if the primary one does not work on the client's current platform. Let's take a look at Figure 3-2.

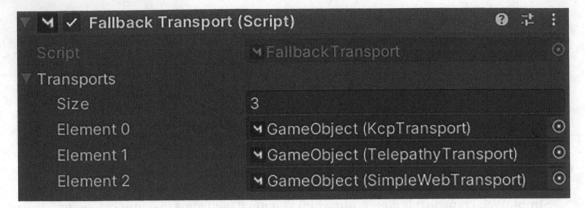

Figure 3-2. *The figure showcases the fallback transport component and its references*

The fallback transport is effortless to use. It simply needs a reference to your primary and additional transport components. We'll go into more detail on setup later in the book. However, it's important to note that the transport layers that you assign to the fallback transport need to be binary compatible with one another, meaning that they need to follow the same conventions and transport data in the same binary format.

Multiplex Transport Component

We also have something called the multiplex transport. The Multiplex Transport is a component that allows a server to "listen" for different transport layers. The Multiplex Transport component enables Mirror Networking to support multiple transport layers on a server level, allowing for virtually total coverage of all platforms, including WebGL. An excellent example of this is using a Multiplex Transport on the server to multiplex a TCP and WebSocket transport layer. This kind of multiplexing would allow your native application clients to connect via TCP while allowing WebGL users to communicate through WebSockets.

Using Encryption, NAT Layers, and Relays

The additional transport component logic allows us to encrypt our data and use NAT punch-through or even use relay servers. The first is essential when dealing with sensitive information or even just things like having players communicate privately. The second is appreciated by players when they're allowed to host their servers or dynamically create lobbies. NAT punch-through allows two devices to connect, while both are behind routers with native address translation enabled.

The IPv4 exhaustion crisis means that almost every consumer device running your game will be behind a NAT-enabled router.

Punch-through or hole punching works by having both parties connect to an unrestricted third party, which stores their connection information such as external and internal IP addresses and ports and then relays that information to the other client. This handover facilitates a direct connection between the two devices without configuring port forwarding on the router.

Encryption Using Monke

Setting up Monke is a straightforward process. However, you will need to enable "Allow 'unsafe' code" in your Unity Player Settings ➤ Player ➤ Other Settings for it to work. Once that's done, you can import the latest UnityPackage from

`https://github.com/cxxpxr/monke/releases`

Monke, is much like other additional transport layer logic components, a drag and drop process.

- Add Monke to your Network Manager.

- Assign Monke as your Transport Layer.

- Assign your usual transport layer to Monke (Figure 3-3).

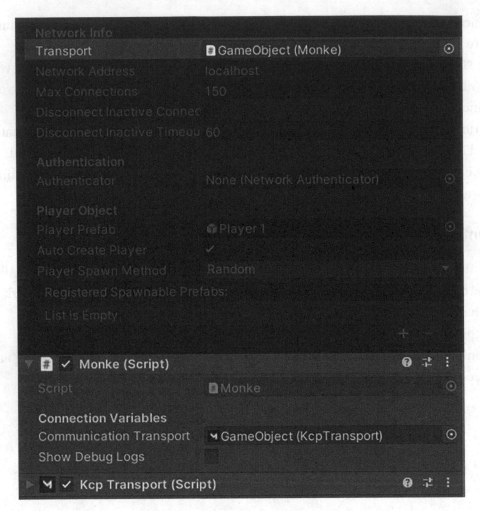

Figure 3-3. *The figure is showcasing the Monke component*

It's important to note that Monke only encrypts outgoing traffic and decrypts incoming traffic. It is not a full-fledged security system, but using Monke is a step you should consider doing.

NAT Punch-Through Using Epic Online Transport

NAT punch-through sounds like the ideal solution, but generally, it has drawbacks. You need access to an accessible third party, which isn't too much of an issue. The main problem is the fact that NAT is very hit or miss. Several ISPs block NAT, and it won't work for cellphone connections.

Thankfully, Epic Games has a server that we can use for precisely this purpose should you decide to attempt a NAT punched connection.

For EoS Transport to work, you'll need to grab yourself an Epic Games developer account and get the Unity SDK and the relevant SDK keys. Once done, add an EoS SDK component to your scene, and fill in the required SDK keys into the inspector window.

Finally, attach the EoS Transport to your Network Manager game object, and assign it as the active transport. It is important to note that multiple instances of your game on one device for testing require multiple epic accounts. Even if your game doesn't use Epic Games accounts, you will need them for testing.

You can get EoS Transport from the following GitHub address:

`https://github.com/FakeByte/EpicOnlineTransport`

The server can then use EOSSDKComponent.LocalUserProductIdString to get a string that you can send to other users to connect to use Mirror Networking.

Relay Using Light-Reflective Mirror

So, if NAT-punched networks are such a hit-and-miss gamble, how can we work around NAT and get our players connecting? Another workaround to punch-throughs is using what's called a relay server.

Layers of Choice

So, what layers would I recommend using? Well, that depends on your needs, but my personal preference would have to be between KCP or Ignorance. These transport layers are compelling, so much so that it's hard to say which one is "the best."

Both can comfortably run 100+ concurrent players without any tweaks. Ignorance has a tiny bit more CPU overhead but also has more channels. They're both reliable transport layers and work out of the box.

As for personal preference, KCP is my favorite and also ships with Mirror Networking. So, for this book, it'll be the transport layer of choice. However, let's discuss both in detail and talk about Telepathy, the default but robust transport layer that ships with Mirror.

KCP – Reliable UDP Transport Layer

So what exactly is KCP?

The KCP transport is a line-by-line translation of a C library of the same name by Skywind3000. Vis2K, the creator of Mirror Networking, wrote the translation, which is now highly used in Mirror. KCP in itself is a unique networking stack in that it can reduce average latency by 30–40%! Yes, you read that right. The downside to this is a slight increase in bandwidth usage, 10–20% to be more precise. This small trade-off can be a huge selling point for this transport layer. Lower latency means happier players.

KCP, at its core, is a UDP-based ARQ (automatic repeat request) protocol, which is a form of error control. The KCP transport is a reliable UDP transport layer featuring two channels, Reliable and Unreliable – and insanely performant networking. KCP ships out of the box with Mirror Networking and is excellent for MMO scale networking.

Pros:

- 30–40% reduced average latency.

- MMO scale networking support.

- Reliable UDP.

- Low CPU overhead.

Cons:

- 10–20% more bandwidth usage.

Overall, KCP is a solid transport layer and is my personal preference.

Ignorance – Reliable UDP Transport Layer

Ignorance is another robust transport layer for Mirror Networking, written by SoftwareGuy. This transport layer goes toe to toe with KCP. While it does have a tiny bit more overhead than KCP, it also supports more channels and a variety of optimization and additional settings for you to tweak.

You can download ignorance from the following GitHub link:
`https://github.com/SoftwareGuy/Ignorance`
Pros:

- MMO scale networking support

- Reliable UDP

- 255 channels

- 4096 max connected peers (theoretical limit)

Cons:

- Marginally more CPU overhead than KCP

Ignorance is bliss, literally.

Telepathy – TCP Transport Layer

Telepathy is the default transport layer that ships with Mirror Networking. Telepathy is the transport layer used in the Mirror Networking examples.

One might assume that the default transport layer wouldn't be great, but you'd be mistaken. It's only marginally worse in performance and is possibly the best TCP transport available to mirror.

Pros:

- It just works.

- Comfortably handles 128+ heavy bandwidth CCU.

"If it ain't broken, why fix it?"

The Client, the Server, and the Host

So now that we've covered a lot of the low-level networking concepts that we'll need, it's time to begin talking about the application level, Mirror Networking itself. When it comes to creating multiplayer games with Mirror Networking, there is a critical distinction that will always need to be on your mind while programming the logic that you will be executing in your game.

That is that despite being a single project, there are two "layers" to your game and a third hybrid "layer." What's vital to understand here is that I'm not talking about layers as you're typically used to in Unity. I'm talking about instances of the game logic.

Let me elaborate. When working with Mirror Networking, you have a client that connects to a server. Two separate application instances: make two builds, run one as a server, then join a client to that game. Simple enough?

Changing a local variable on the client does not mean that the variable will change on the server. The client needs to make a networked request to the server to change a variable and then listen for that change. This back and forth is how a networked game operates. In almost all instances, the server should not trust the client.

Then, we have a third, the host. The host is a unique hybrid. It is like a server but also behaves like a client. Think of it as internally running a server, then connecting to that internal server and playing as the client because a host is more of a client than a server.

The Client

The client is the endpoint that your players use to connect to a multiplayer game. It represents the best approximation of the game's current state on the server, letting your players interact with hundreds of other players.

Think of the client like a single-player game session. But, instead, parts of the game world reflect what's happening on the server. That's Mirror Networking in a nutshell. The goal is to create the most accurate representation of the game state on the server while minimizing latency and reducing the risk of cheating.

As such, the client, in most cases, is almost exclusively an observer, with minimal ways of affecting the states of objects on the server. Any interaction with the world should generally be asking the server to have the server affect the game world. This authoritative structure can vary depending on your needs and game server architecture, but you should generally authoritatively develop your games. We'll discuss game server architecture in the next chapter. In the meantime, let's have a deeper look at the server.

The Server

The server is the workhorse of a Mirror Network. It is the matrix and controls the actual authoritative state of objects. The server should own the game-state of all dynamic objects in the game world that matter. The goal is to have the server control the rules, execute the logic that defines how objects change, and simply replicate the results back to the connected players.

Say you have a barrel that you deem needs to explode. The barrel exists on the game server as a game object. It has a component called BarrelLogic and a network identity that identifies it on the network. This barrel and its identity are replicated by mirror over the network to your clients, A and B.

Client A will ask the server to destroy the barrel. Then the server will receive that request over the mirror network. Based on a set of rules, the server then decides if player A should be allowed to have the barrel destroyed. If the server deems that the barrel must go, it sends a message back to all connected players, notifying them that the barrel needs to explode. When client B receives the message from the server, they play the barrel's explode animation. Shortly after, the server notifies all clients that the barrel no longer exists and can be safely destroyed.

We'll discuss more how this back and forth works in the next chapter, but for now, all you need to know is that the server controls the state of the game and reflects the server's state to the connected clients.

The Host

In the beginning, the host is something that many developers struggle with when learning Mirror Networking. What exactly is it, though? Hosting allows you to play your game and have other players connect to you, which can be very useful for specific genres of games. However, here's the part that most developers miss in the beginning. The host is, in fact, not a new type of player. It is simply a client connecting internally to an internally hosted server.

As such, it's important to note that the host instance will not have authority over other objects in the game world. Because the game state is not running on the host, it's running on the internal server, with the host simply being another client connected to that server.

So, always treat a host like a client. I'd even go as far as to recommend not using host mode at all until you're more familiar with the structure of Mirror. It's far easier to debug when you isolate the server and the client. Nevertheless, host mode can be great once you're familiar with the Mirror Networking environment.

The host mode is excellent for letting your players seamlessly host and play with their friends without the need for a dedicated client (Figure 3-4).

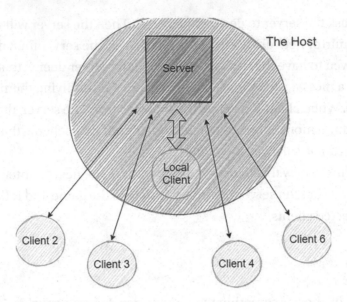

Figure 3-4. *The architecture of a host, internally, is just a client connected to a server*

The Network Manager

The network manager is the entry point for Mirror. It's also likely the first component that you'll interact with when working with Mirror Networking. The network manager is responsible for hosting a mirror server or connecting to a mirror server. It also has a wide variety of configuration settings. Let's take a look at Figure 3-5.

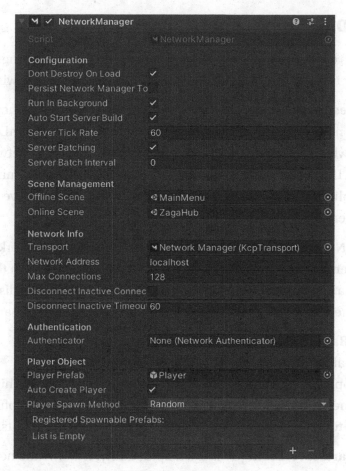

Figure 3-5. *The figure shows the Network Manager component within Mirror Networking*

As you can see, there are plenty of configuration options for us to tweak. Let's examine each section and explore what each option does and how it affects our networked environment.

Configuration

The first section is configuration. Here, we can specify the general settings for our network manager that define how it should behave. These are the following:

- **DontDestroyOnLoad** - This boolean value determines whether or not the network manager should move to the DontDestroyOnLoad scene, which will result in the network manager persisting between scenes. If you don't check this, you will require a network manager in your online and offline scenes. Generally, it's excellent to leave this setting enabled.

- **PersistNetworkManagerToOfflineScene** - Should the network manager be kept when loading to the offline scene, such as in the case of a disconnect? Generally speaking, you can leave this disabled since the offline scene will typically contain a new network manager.

- **RunInBackground** - This is a crucial setting that you should almost always leave enabled. Without this setting enabled, if your application loses focus, you will lose your connection. This disconnecting when the application loses focus could be helpful in some situations, such as within niche enterprise environments.

- **AutoStartServerBuild** - This is a helpful utility. It allows the network manager to detect if it's running as a server build automatically. If it sees itself as a server build, it can then automatically start hosting a server.

- **ServerTickRate** - The current tick rate that the server should use.

- **ServerBatching** - Server batching allows you to reduce your networking overhead by sending all of your messages during LateUpdate or after a batch interval if you have set one.

- **ServerBatchInterval** - Optionally assign an interval to use for server batching instead of sending messages every late update.

These settings are beneficial, so be sure to familiarize yourself with them.

Scene Management

Next, we have the scene management settings. These are useful for automatically handling a scene transition when connecting or disconnecting from the Mirror Network:

- **OfflineScene** - If assigned, the client will automatically load this server in the event of going offline or disconnecting from the Mirror Network. The network manager simply internally listens to the OnDisconnect event. Switching to the offline scene on disconnect helps redirect players to a disconnect or main menu screen when they lose connection to your servers.

- **OnlineScene** - The online scene is much like the offline scene, but instead of redirecting on disconnect, it loads the online scene when the player successfully connects to the Mirror Network.

Network Info

Networking info is where we give Mirror Networking information on how the network should work, such as what transport layer to use and parameters such as maximum player count and the host address to connect to when running as a client. Let's see these in detail. It's important to note that the last two properties, DisconnectInactiveConnections and DisconnectInactiveTimeout, are obsolete and now responsible for the transport itself.

- **Transport** - This property specifies what transport Mirror Networking should use for this instance of the game. Generally speaking, transports are binary compatible, meaning each transport layer should have the same binary message. This binary compatibility means that the server can use a different transport to the client. Binary compatibility is the standard best practice when developing new transport layers, so bear in mind that some may not adhere to this standard.

- **NetworkAddress** - This parameter specifies what address clients should connect to when calling StartClient.

- **MaxConnections** - The maximum number of concurrent network connections to allow; a connection counts toward that limit after the NetworkServer.OnTransportConnected event.

- **DisconnectInactiveConnections** - This is an obsolete option that is now the responsibility of your chosen transport.

- **DisconnectInactiveTimeout** - Much like DisconnectInactiveConnections, this option is now obsolete and is the responsibility of your transport.

Authentication – Network Authenticator

When you first start with Mirror, a simple host and connect setup will suffice. However, as you move on to larger projects, chances are that data persistence will begin to play a more significant and more prominent role in how your players interact with your game and your servers. For this persistence, we typically use databases to store data associated with a given player, but how can we trust that the player is who they say they are? The simple answer is never trust your players. If a connection tells you that they are John, you don't let them in until you've validated that they are indeed John.

But if clients can simply join a hosted server, how do we stop them from entering directly, and how do we authenticate that the connection is who they say they are if we can't trust them? The answer is the Network Authenticator. Let's take a look at an example implementation called the basic authenticator (Figure 3-6).

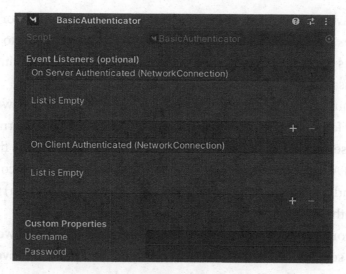

Figure 3-6. *The figure is an example implementation of NetworkAuthenticator*

Now, it's essential to understand that the Network Authenticator is very versatile and adaptable. Generally speaking, you wouldn't use BasicAuthenticator in a production release. BasicAuthenticator is simply an example of how to use and inherit from Network Authenticator. Let's take a deeper look at the basic authenticator before digging into how we can create our network authenticator to meet the needs of our project.

The basic authenticator is very, well, basic. It provides an example of a plaintext username and password validation system. First, we have the exposed events. These are as follows.

OnServerAuthenticated

This event becomes invoked when the client successfully becomes accepted by the server as authenticated. This event can be listened to by entities on the mirror network and helps notify such entities that the server successfully authenticated the client. The server itself typically uses the OnServerAuthenticated event, but other players can use the event to see that their friend has successfully authenticated.

OnClientAuthenticated

Much like the OnServerAuthenticated event, the OnClientAuthenticated is an evet invoked once the server has successfully authenticated the client connection. However, instead of affecting listeners on the Mirror Network, this event is an event that is invoked on the client requesting authentication. The OnClientAuthenticated event is ideal for displaying UI elements notifying the user that their login was successful.

Finally, we have some custom properties, the username and password fields. This example uses a plaintext authenticator. When the client connects to the server, the client requests authentication by sending a network message containing the AuthRequestMessage.

This AuthRequestMessage includes the client's username and password and gets sent to the server for authentication. The server then compares the username and password to its username and password fields. If the fields are a match, the server responds with an AuthResponseMessage. The AuthResponseMessage contains a response code and a message. The server then calls ServerAccept(conn) to mark the connection as authenticated.

Now, in no world would a game server only have one account that we can log in with, let alone sharing sensitive information like a username and password over the Internet in plaintext. The basic authenticator is only an example.

We should always create our authenticators to match the needs of our project, and there are multiple ways of going about authentication. Let's see how we can make our authenticator.

Custom Network Authentication

There are several ways for us to handle custom network authentication. You could use a username and password authentication system and encrypt the traffic using Monke. However, a better approach would be to use something like OAuth. Let's take a look at a few methods of authenticating our users.

Generic Username and Password Authentication

While on paper, using a generic username and password authentication seems simple; it can become complicated as your product grows and starts to get attention. This difficulty comes along because authenticating a user's password requires you to have their password stored securely.

Typically, this is done by never actually holding the user's password itself. Instead, you keep an encrypted hash of their password, and you then compare these hashes to validate that the passwords match. The complexity comes from the legalities and regulations involved in storing sensitive user information.

These regulations can vary from country to country, and while a small new game is likely not going to gain any negative attention, it should be your primary goal to keep your users safe from malicious actors.

Authenticating Users Using OAuth2 and an OpenID Provider

OAuth2 is an industry-leading authorization protocol that ensures that your user's passwords remain safe for the authentication process. This high level of security is possible because, during the authentication process, the user's password never passes through your system. It also frees us from the responsibility of keeping our user's passwords safe, as well as the legislations that come with it. We use OAuth2 as the authorization protocol and OpenID as the authentication protocol, allowing us to authorize and authenticate our users.

OpenID and OAuth2 work together with a third-party identity provider, such as Google, Facebook, Amazon, and others, to provide additional information about your users. The great thing about this is that it enables users to log into your application with their Google or Facebook accounts. On top of this, Google and Facebook have APIs to provide us with more information about the user, with the user's consent.

Let's look at Figure 3-7 to get an idea of how OAuth and OpenID work to provide us with such a robust authentication solution.

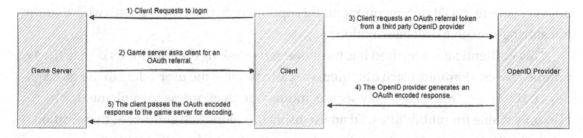

Figure 3-7. *The figure demonstrates the authorization and authentication of an OAuth2 and OpenID system*

First, the user requests to connect to our game server; this passes through our custom authenticator.

Before we can let the user fully connect to our server and proceed, we need them to provide us with an OAuth referral response, which we can use to authenticate the user. We send that request to the user, and we redirect the user to a third-party OpenID provider, such as Facebook or Google.

After that, the client logs into their Facebook or Google account on the respective third-party provider's website. Optionally, we can include a request for additional information, like their name, surname, email address, and other information we might need for our game. The user then agrees to share this information with us.

Next, the OAuth provider gives the client an encoded response, which the client, in turn, gives to us to decode. The ended response is then validated, and once we're happy that the client is who they say they are, we accept them with our authenticator, and they connect to the game server.

Using OAuth and OpenID is a great way to handle authentication, and I'd highly recommend taking this route, especially when creating mobile titles or social games.

Using a Third Party Such as Steam or Epic Games

Another excellent option for authentication is using the SDKs provided by Steam or Epic Games. These SDKs allow you to implement Steam or Epic Games login into your game client.

The SDK enables your users to log in with their Steam or Epic Games account and is exceptionally convenient. If you're developing a desktop title releasing on Epic Games or Steam, then I'd highly recommend using this option.

Using the Device ID of the Mobile Device

Using the device ID is a popular authentication route for mobile games but is also not very secure. So I'd only recommend this option for hyper-casual games where you're not storing sensitive user information.

This authentication method has the game server asking the user for its device ID, a unique device identifier. Once obtained, we can associate the user's data to the given device ID. Again, this is not a very secure option, but it's effortless to implement. It's also only viable for mobile titles. I'd advise using this alongside another authentication method, allowing users to migrate their data in situations where they obtain a new device.

Creating Our Custom Network Authenticator

Now that we understand a couple of authentication methods available to us, let's explore creating our custom network authenticator.

To create our custom network authenticator, we'll need to create a class that derives from the abstract class, Authenticator. Alongside this requirement, we also need to subscribe to the OnAuthRequestMessage handler.

Thankfully, Mirror Networking has made this incredibly easy. You can have the editor generate a framework for you to use for your custom authenticator (Figure 3-8).

Firstly, navigate your asset browser to the location that you'd like to save the class. For my example, I'll navigate to Assets/Core/Authentication.

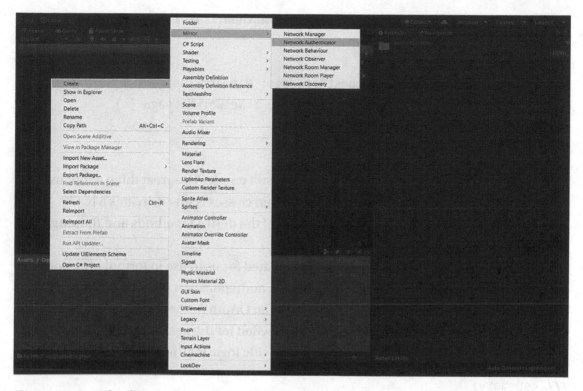

Figure 3-8. *The figure shows how to create a custom network authenticator class*

Once I've navigated my asset browser to the location of my choice, I right-click in the asset browser window to bring up the context menu. From there, I can navigate to Create ➤ Mirror ➤ Network Authenticator.

Clicking this option will create a new class that I can give a name of my choice. At the end of this chapter, I'll detail creating a custom network authenticator using OAuth and Google. So, I'll name this class OAuthAuthenticator.

Let's open the newly created class.

```
/*
Authenticators:
https://mirror-networking.com/docs/Components/Authenticators/
Documentation:
https://mirror-networking.com/docs/Guides/Authentication.html
API Reference: https://mirror-networking.com/docs/api/Mirror.
NetworkAuthenticator.html
*/
```

```
public class OAuthAuthenticator : NetworkAuthenticator
    {
        #region Messages
        public struct AuthRequestMessage : NetworkMessage { }
        public struct AuthResponseMessage : NetworkMessage { }
        #endregion
...
```

The first thing you'll notice is that the class isn't empty. The great thing about using the context menu to create Mirror-specific derived classes is that it creates a really neat framework class to work with, showing all of the derived methods and thoroughly commenting on them.

Next, we have two empty structs that are created for us to use in formulating our requests and responses that we'll use during the authentication process. During the chapter exercise, we'll go into detail on creating an OAuth Authenticator using Facebook. We'll modify these structs to contain the data needed for the authentication process. Next up, we have a region containing the server-side logic for the authentication process.

```
/// <summary>
/// Called on server from StartServer to initialize the Authenticator
/// <para> Server message handlers should be registered in this method.
    </para>
/// </summary>

  public override void OnStartServer()
  {
    // Register a handler for the authentication request we expect
    // from client.
    NetworkServer.RegisterHandler<AuthRequestMessage>(OnAuthRequestMessage ,
    false);
  }
```

In OnStartServer, it's vital that we register a handler for the AuthRequestMessage that we're expecting to get from our clients and we mark the handler as not requiring authentication by passing false as the second argument. We don't want the handle to require authentication because at this point in time, the user won't be authenticated yet.

```
/// <summary>
/// Called on server from OnServerAuthenticateInternal when a client needs
    to
/// authenticate
/// </summary>
/// <param name="conn">Connection to client.</param>

  public override void OnServerAuthenticate(NetworkConnection conn) { }
```

The OnServerAuthenticate, not to be confused with OnServerAuthenticated, gets called internally when a client needs to authenticate. Generally, we don't have a need for this, so we can either remove it from our class or ignore it.

There are some use cases though, such as prematurely rejecting an auth request based on IP region.

```
/// <summary>
/// Called on server when the client's AuthRequestMessage arrives
/// </summary>
/// <param name="conn">Connection to client.</param>
/// <param name="msg">The message payload</param>
  public void OnAuthRequestMessage(NetworkConnection conn,
  AuthRequestMessage msg)
      {
          AuthResponseMessage authResponseMessage = new
          AuthResponseMessage();
          conn.Send(authResponseMessage);

          // Accept the successful authentication
          ServerAccept(conn);
      }
```

Next, importantly, we have the OnAuthRequestMessage. This gets fired when the client sends us an AuthRequestMessage. We can then use that AuthRequestMessage to authenticate the user. We should handle authentication here and then either call ServerAccept(conn) to accept the given connection as authenticated or call ServerReject(conn) to reject the authentication request and notify the user that their request was rejected.

That covers it for the server-side code. It's really easy to use and simple to extend upon.

Then, we have the client-side code.

```
/// <summary>
/// Called on client from StartClient to initialize the Authenticator
/// <para>Client message handlers should be registered in this method.</
    para>
/// </summary>
  public override void OnStartClient()
      {
          // register a handler for the authentication response we expect
              from
          // server.
          NetworkClient.RegisterHandler<AuthResponseMessage>(OnAuthRespon
          seMessage,
          false);
      }
```

Again, much like with the server, we need to register a handler, but this time to the AuthResponseMessage so we know to do something when we receive our response from the server. We should register this handler in OnStartClient.

```
/// <summary>
/// Called on client from OnClientAuthenticateInternal when a client needs
    to
/// authenticate
/// </summary>
/// <param name="conn">Connection of the client.</param>
  public override void OnClientAuthenticate(NetworkConnection conn)
      {
          AuthRequestMessage authRequestMessage = new
          AuthRequestMessage();

          NetworkClient.Send(authRequestMessage);
      }
```

Then, we have the OnClientAuthenticate. This is called when the client needs to authenticate. It's a lot more useful on the client; we can use this to bring up a login dialogue, redirect the user to an OAuth page, or formulate our AuthRequestMessage.

We then send the AuthRequestMessage using NetworkClient.Send() with the struct containing our auth data.

```
/// <summary>
/// Called on client when the server's AuthResponseMessage arrives
/// </summary>
/// <param name="conn">Connection to client.</param>
/// <param name="msg">The message payload</param>
  public void OnAuthResponseMessage(AuthResponseMessage msg)
      {
          // Authentication has been accepted
          ClientAccept(NetworkClient.connection);
      }
```

Last but not least, we have the OnAuthResponseMessage. This is where we handle the response received from the server. We can use this to notify the user of any errors, such as invalid data, or begin an onboarding process if it's the user's first time playing.

That covers the NetworkAuthenticator; I'll be going through how to create an OAuth authenticator in the exercise section, so be sure to follow that to see how I handle OAuth through Google.

Player Object

Next up in the Network Manager, we have fields relating to the PlayerObject. These fields are as follows:

- **PlayerObject** - This field allows Mirror Networking to spawn a prefab for the player's connection and give the associated connection authority over that player.

- **AutoCreatePlayer** - If enabled, Mirror Networking will spawn the player prefab upon having the player connect to the server.

- **PlayerSpawnMethod** - Specifies if Mirror Networking should spawn the player at random NetworkStart locations or in a round-robin style. For this to work, you need to have game objects in the scene with a NetworkStart component.

Registered Spawnable Prefabs

The registered spawnable prefabs is a list of manually registered prefabs that are allowed to be spawned during runtime. These can be assigned automatically too using a different process that we'll cover later in this book. For now, it's important to note that any prefab not in the scene file needs to be registered in this list if you intend to instantiate and spawn the prefab during the game. We'll cover spawning networked objects later in the book.

Network Identities

Network identities are the heart of Mirror Networking; they're used to identify objects over the network. If something needs to be networked, it needs a network identity. More importantly, a network identity cannot be a child of another networking identity. This is important to know, as future versions of Mirror will outright stop this from happening. So, it's best to keep any networking logic on the root of your networked prefab, along with its network identity. It's also important to note that any network identities that exist in the scene, before a server exists and is connected to, will be disabled by Unity. This is important because executing logic in Awake will cause the logic to execute, then have the object spawned, potentially destroying some logic that was initialized in Awake and not calling awake again. So, it's best to avoid Awake for any components attached to a network object. Instead, have your class derive from NetworkBehaviour, and call public void override OnStartClient. We'll discuss network behaviors later in the book when we go into more detail on the coding behind creating multiplayer games using Mirror Networking.

Summary

In this chapter, we learned about Mirror Networking and different networking architectures, transport layers, as well as the server, client, and host. We also learned about the network manager and how to configure a multiplayer environment. We then dove into authentication, player objects, and registering spawnable prefabs.

In the next chapter, we'll discuss the chain of command and get a solid understanding of authority and how it impacts the way that you build a multiplayer game using Mirror.

EXERCISE 1 – CREATING A CUSTOM OAUTH2 AUTHENTICATOR USING GOOGLE

So, we're looking to build a custom authenticator using Google login. The standard route to do this would be to use Google's SDK; however, if you're looking to develop something that also supports desktop, you'll encounter a certain hurdle. As of writing, Google's SDK does not support native unity desktop applications.

In order to build a login flow for the desktop build target, you would need to build an entirely custom login flow using the player's browser, and then intercept the web response.

Since there are no guides available for doing this in Unity, let alone Mirror, I'll show you how to create that custom login flow. It's worth noting that the same concept could apply to Facebook. However, and this is a big one, Facebook's redirects need to redirect to an SSL-encrypted endpoint through https. This means that redirecting to client local hosts is not feasible. You will need to host an authentication site to receive any redirects if you plan to use this route.

Let's get started. There are a few things that we'll need to set up first before we begin:

Step 1 – To begin, we'll need to register a new app through Google's API developer portal. In order to do this, you'll need to navigate to `https://console.cloud.google.com/apis/dashboard` and log in. Add an app, and follow the prompts.

Step 2 – Next, you'll want to create an API oAuth 2 client ID to use; you can do this by going to `https://console.cloud.google.com/apis/credentials` and ensuring that your project is selected in the top bar (Figure 3-9).

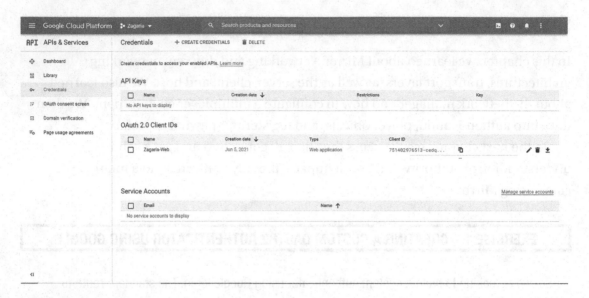

Figure 3-9. *The image shows how the credentials API screen looks and highlights key points of interest*

Step 3 – Next, we want to create an OAuth 2.0 Client ID. You can do this by navigating to Create Credentials ➤ OAuth Client ID. Then, choose the Web Application type, since we'll technically be authenticating via a website authentication call.

Step 4 – Give the new Client ID a memorable name; this name doesn't really matter as it simply identifies the client ID within the console. Something like ApplicationName-Web is a great choice, with application name being the name of your application.

Step 5 – Add http://localhost/ to your authorized redirect URI list. Be sure to include the trailing forward slash. Save your changes by clicking the large Save button at the bottom of the screen.

Step 6 – On the right-hand side of the screen, take note of the Client ID and Client Secret; we'll be using these later.

Step 7 – Time to grab the code; look for GoogleDesktop.cs in my personal authentication repository on GitHub, here: `https://github.com/VoidFletcher/MirrorAuthenticators/`. You can also download the unity package from the releases page.

Step 8 – Attach the authenticator script to a GameObject in your scene, and drag a reference to the authenticator into the Network Manager's Authenticator variable. I typically attach the script directly to my network behavior:

Step 10 – Fill in the authenticator variables; the AppID you took note of earlier should go into the Web App Id field, and the Client Secret should go into the Client Secret field.

Step 11 – Expand the Google scopes list to allow for three entries, and add the following three entries into the list:

- openid

- www.googleapis.com/auth/userinfo.email

- www.googleapis.com/auth/userinfo.profile

Scopes allow you to request specific information; be sure to check out https://developers.google.com/identity/protocols/oauth2/scopes for a list of available scopes.

Step 12 – Run the mirror project, then click Host. Once hosting, you'll attempt to connect to your own server, resulting in an authentication step. Your web browser should open with a Google account selection dialogue (Figure 3-10). Once the dialogue is completed, you'll be prompted to return to the game.

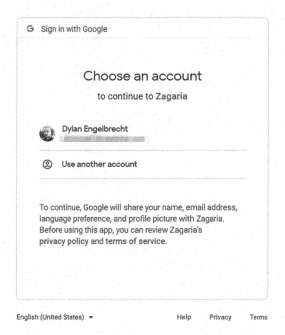

Figure 3-10. *The image shows how the oAuth dialogue looks like*

Step 13 – In game, you'll be accepted into the server, and your logs should display the debug logs, containing some of your account information (Figure 3-11). Remember to remove these in a production environment.

Figure 3-11. *The image shows some of our user information*

There you have it – Google login working for your Mirror Network. I'll cover how to associate the player's data to an account later in the book.

CHAPTER 4

The Chain of Command

By this point, we're starting to understand how to get Mirror up and running for our project, but we haven't covered moving players around yet, interacting with the world or even interacting with other players. So, in this chapter, I'll be covering how to bring your networked product to life.

First, we need to understand a concept called authority. Then, I'll discuss typical game server architectures, which dictate who has authority over objects and players in your game. Next, I'll delve deeper into concepts that allow us to execute remote commands or relay information between players. We'll also cover ways to improve performance and annoy cheaters with interest management. Finally, I'll explain how Mirror's callbacks work, the order of their events, and more.

Finally, we'll build our first multiplayer game. Let's get started.

Authority

Authority, by definition, is *"the power or right to give orders, make decisions, and enforce obedience."* In Mirror Networking and many other networking solutions, regardless of engine, authority is no different from this definition.

We use authority to determine who or what can control an object and values or execute code. Authority is a property of the network identity attached to an object. Any script which interacts with the network needs to be attached to the same game object as the network identity. In the previous chapter, I covered how network identities are the identifiers for game objects on the network. It also acts to keep track of authority when our scripts inherit from NetworkBehaviour, which we'll discuss later in this chapter. Any script inheriting from NetworkBehaviour will have a "hasAuthority" boolean. The network behavior returns the authority value of the attached network identity, which is a great way to check if you have authority over that object.

Internally, the value looks like this:

© Dylan Engelbrecht 2022
D. Engelbrecht, *Building Multiplayer Games in Unity*, https://doi.org/10.1007/978-1-4842-7474-3_4

```
/// <summary>True if this object is the authoritative player object on the
/// client.</summary>
// Determined at runtime. For most objects, authority is held by the server.
// For objects that had their authority set by AssignClientAuthority on
// the server, this will be true on the client that owns the object. NOT
// on other clients.
public bool hasAuthority { get; internal set; }
```

Only a connection with authority over an object may issue commands to the server or move the object's position, rotation, or scale. Network connections that do not have authority over an object will only affect the object locally, and changes will not replicate to other players or servers.

Authority is a great way to prevent cheaters from performing actions like setting other players' health to zero. With that said, though, authority in itself can't stop cheating entirely, and you should actively seek out different forms of anti-cheat. Instead, see authority as a method of preventing conflicting values or commands from being sent to an object, which might cause undesired effects. And view the nuisance it causes to cheaters as a benefit.

There is no way to stop cheaters completely. There are, however, ways to mitigate the damage that they can do to your game or community, detect cheating, and punish or remove the cheaters from the game.

When building online multiplayer games, it's vital to consider the architecture of your networking code, when and how players affect the game world, and balance the pros and cons of different architectures to find a balance that works for you and most of your players' base. Let's discuss what exactly game server architecture is and where it fits into the picture of building multiplayer games with Mirror.

Game Server Architecture

Game networking has a concept called game server architecture. This architecture represents almost a design pattern of how messages should flow between your players and servers. Each architecture contains its pros and cons, depending entirely on the product you're trying to build. While Mirror Networking uses an indeterministic client-server model, I'll cover each of the most common networking architectures, how they work, and why they work. I'll also explain the cons of each networking architecture.

So why are there so many models? The sad truth about that is the direct consequence of some of your players, the cheaters. Cheaters will always be around and will always jump at the opportunity of playing by their own rules. Cheaters cheat for their gain or simply the gratification of ruining another player's experience.

Game server architecture helps tackle the overall design of your networking to mitigate cheating or, in the case where you don't care if there are cheaters, like a local co-op game, to improve the player experience. Thus, architecture is a design philosophy that you should think through before even writing your first line of network code, keeping in mind time versus effort versus reward.

Input vs. State-Based Architecture

When we build a multiplayer game, what exactly are we replicating over the network? One might think this would be a simple question to ask, but it can depend entirely on your game or product, the genre, and what needs the architecture should fulfill.

That brings me to the topic of input- or state-based replication. Let's first cover what exactly I mean when I say that. When you use an input-based replication system, we send the player's inputs through the network, such as a "PlayerPressedForwardInput()" command.

On the other hand,, if we're using a state-based architecture, we send the positional values over the network instead of sending the movement input itself. Each of these approaches has its place in networked game server architecture. We can use input replication, or state-based replication, or a combination of both, in our game server architecture. Each of these approaches has its place in networked game server architecture. Our choice depends on whether or not our network simulation is deterministic or not.

Input-Based Replication – Pros and Cons

Typically, the pros and cons of these different forms of replication depend on the architecture itself since some of these may change. However, in general, input-based replication has the following pros and cons:

Pros

- **Typically has significantly lower bandwidth usage** - This is since you're only invoking movement and interaction commands. Furthermore, in a deterministic environment, you won't even need to replicate any values.

- **It can work great in an entirely authoritative server architecture** -
  This works great in an RTS or MOBA context. However, the fully
  authoritative approach, in combination with other techniques, can
  make cheating extremely difficult.

Cons

- **Generally requires deterministic logic** - Deterministic logic is
  typically needed if using a pure input-based replication architecture
  which can be a hassle to build and implement.

- **Harder to reconnect** - In a deterministic game architecture, you'll
  need to resync all events from the start of the game session to a
  reconnecting player, making implementation quite a pain since you'll
  need to build a recording system to store the entire session.

Input-based replication has its place, but keep in mind that it can require significant
additional work, time, and effort to implement correctly.

Let's take a look at state-based replication.

State-Based Replication – Pros and Cons

Typically, when building multiplayer games with Mirror, we'll be using state-based
replication. It's generally a breeze to develop for, and bandwidth generally isn't an issue
if you're not going crazy with your replication.

Let's take a look at some of the pros and cons of this state-based replication.

Pros

- **Harder to cheat** - Since state-based replications overwrite values
  when the client receives them, it can make cheating a lot harder.

- **Easy to reconnect dropped clients** - Since we're anyway
  synchronizing the states of all networked objects, a player can simply
  reconnect and receive all of the current values and then continue as if
  nothing happened.

- **Works excellently in indeterministic environments** - Since we
  can use an indeterministic approach, the development effort is
  significantly lower.

Cons

- **Limited architecture support** - It can be a hassle to get this kind of replication to work well in lockstep architectures.

Overall, I prefer using state-based replication where possible. Not only does Mirror Networking work great with state-based replication, but it's also just straightforward. However, it's essential to know how both work and be willing to use the replication that best suits your game's needs.

Deterministic vs. Indeterministic Architecture

Another key point when deciding your architecture is to understand the difference between deterministic and indeterministic networking. When talking about determinism with network architecture, what we're saying is, "If I flip a coin 100 times, will I get the same results if I flip the coin another 100 times." In a deterministic network, the coins will always land in the same order. However, logic dictates that if we flip a coin a hundred times, chances are that the coin order will be different. That's because physics is generally indeterministic. Deterministic systems, depending on the complexity of your game or product, can be complicated and time-consuming to build.

The idea with deterministic architecture is to record every action that each player takes and play those actions back, yielding the same networked game simulation every time.

Recording and playing back these actions are great for recording game sessions or even, in combination with a fully authoritative lockstep architecture, a way to minimize cheating.

The problem with deterministic systems is their complexity, and complexity is time, money, and resources. Using a deterministic network architecture without using a fully authoritative server is also a breeding ground for cheaters.

Having everything run on a fully authoritative server can be a problem with deterministic systems, as players will feel latency since we must send every input to the server, which is no problem if you're playing a game of chess, but if you're trying to aim around a corner in a first-person shooter game, this can become a problem. Another con of deterministic systems is that Unity and Mirror Networking do not support it out of the box. Instead, Unity and Mirror networking work best with indeterministic networking using state-based synchronization. That's no saying it's not possible to do deterministic networking in Mirror Networking. Still, you will encounter other struggles if you decide to take that approach, again, depending on the complexity of your game.

So, my personal preference here is taking an indeterministic approach when working with Mirror Networking.

Peer-to-Peer

Peer-to-peer networking is when two or more players connect, typically with one of the players becoming a host. This architecture has the advantage of not needing to host any dedicated servers for your players.

However, that also means that the architecture is easy to cheat in most cases. This vulnerability to cheating is generally not an issue, though, as peer-to-peer architecture is generally better suited to small-scale co-op games (less than 16 players). With these games, it's typically difficult for players to ruin the game experience for other players. The isolation of cheating is possible since the only players that the cheaters can interact with are the people in their small, isolated session, typically friends.

Friends can be an excellent cheating deterrent in itself since players typically value their friends more than being able to gain an unfair advantage against a stranger. In addition, since strangers are not involved, cheating diminishes. However, if you plan to have item persistence between game sessions and players, it would still be wise to limit the impact of cheating, especially if items are tradable or have perceived value.

Let's take a look at what a peer-to-peer network looks like at a conceptual level (Figure 4-1).

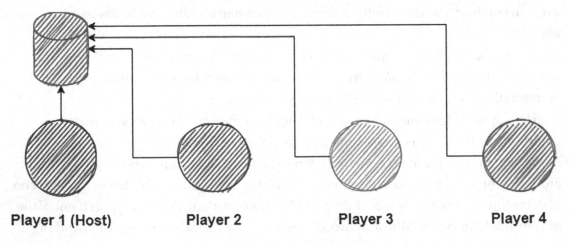

Player 1 (Host)   **Player 2**   **Player 3**   **Player 4**

Figure 4-1. *The figure showcases a typical peer-to-peer game network session*

The modern peer-to-peer network in itself draws a lot of likeness to the client-server model that we'll discuss shortly.

First, however, the server gets hosted by a player. In this configuration, one of the players, typically the first player, becomes a host. Then, the rest of the players connect to that hosting player.

Mirror networking uses the client-server model exclusively. However, a modern approach to peer-to-peer networking, like the recent example, is possible with Mirror Networking and is relatively easy to implement.

In older architectures, such as lockstep, all players connect to all other players. This configuration is more faithful to the nature of peer-to-peer. Still, it typically requires a deterministic server architecture to be followed, which can be extremely difficult and time-consuming to build. Mirror itself is a client-server model and does not support older architectures, which is not an issue since it doesn't need to.

When building small-scale co-op games with Mirror Networking, you'll want to take the first approach and allow one of your players to become the host for their friends to connect.

So, what happens if the hosting player disconnects? In situations like these, you can either terminate the game session, allowing players to save the current game state and exit, or, even better, reconnect them. But, if the host is no longer available, how do we reconnect the other players? The answer is host migration.

Host migration is an excellent pattern that allows dropped clients to communicate with one another, establish a new host, and continue the game. Unfortunately, Mirror Networking does not support true host migration out of the box, but we can implement the concept.

However, this implementation's difficulty varies significantly based on the game's complexity and the game state. So, let's take a look at how we could approach a pseudo-host migration.

If we look at Figure 4-2, we can see that the original host, player 1, has lost connection to the rest of the players. Since the other players can no longer connect to the host, they instead fall back to another host, player 3.

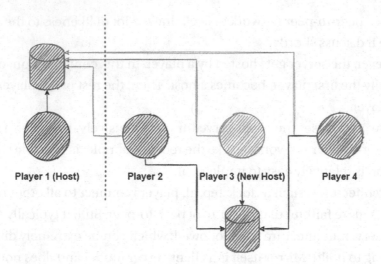

Figure 4-2. *The figure demonstrates a host migration*

Now, Mirror doesn't support this out of the box. To achieve host migration, we should have player connections stored on the server and available to other players. During regular gameplay, the server should query players to find an open port and ensure that we can make a connection. After finding a prime candidate, the address and port should be available to all players as a fallback address.

The host player should store all state values of the game, then begin hosting a new session. Players will then connect to that session, and the host will revert networked objects to their saved states. During this state revert, it can become complex, depending on the number of networked states and the complexity of the data. Players then restore their positions and continue the game session. Mirror Networking recommends that you should hide this transition behind a UI to make the player experience smoother.

To summarize, the process should look something like Figure 4-3.

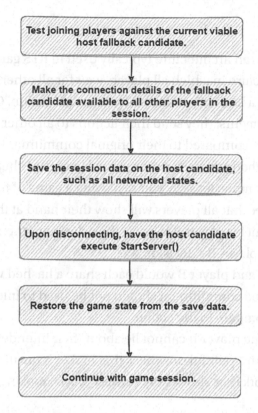

Figure 4-3. *Figure 4-3 summarizes the process of creating a pseudo-host migration*

The peer-to-peer architecture, or at least the pseudo-peer-to-peer architecture, is overall an excellent choice. It's impressive because it leverages Mirror Networking's client-server structure and makes it more dynamic, perfect for saving costs and quickly implementing multiplayer co-op into your game or product.

Here are some games that work on this architecture:

True Peer-to-Peer Games

- Demigod - A MOBA developed by Gas Powered Games back in 2009.

Pseudo-Peer-to-Peer

- Borderlands

- Overcooked

- Satisfactory

So, it's worth keeping this architecture in mind, especially for small-scale networking games, especially co-op games that friends might play together.

Lockstep

Lockstep networking was an architecture typically used in RTS games in the late 1990s. It's a networking architecture in which all players wait for all other player commitments. These commitments are a hashed version of the intended action. Once the players receive all other commitments, they send their actions to all other players. This action must then be hashed and compared to their original commitment.

This networking method solves some issues with a type of cheating known as "Look-Ahead Cheating." For example, let's say you're playing a game of rock, paper, scissors, but you cannot guarantee that all players will show their hand at the same time. Player A could, for example, wait for player B to show their decision, then show their own decision, knowing what player B's decision was.

In lockstep, player A and player B would each share a hashed version of the commitment. This hashed commitment should not be used to infer the action directly but should also easily compare to the action.

That way, player A and player B cannot lie about their intended actions. Lockstep does, however, come with a painful drawback that makes it unsuitable for most modern games. The entire network is as slow as the slowest player, making it unsuitable for many games and genres.

As such, the last bastion of lockstep networking was likely RTS games. But, even then, there was another drawback. Lockstep typically requires a fully deterministic networking architecture, and due to the complexity and difficulty associated with lockstep networking, we usually abandon it in favor of the client-server model.

True Lockstep Games

- Supreme Commander 1

- Warcraft 3

- Doom

Pseudo-lockstep (Lockstep with Client-Server Model)

- Starcraft 2

Client-Server Architecture

Client-Server Architecture – this is where we come in. Mirror Networking uses a pure client-server model. While, in theory, you could extend Mirror Networking to use a different model, there are very few reasons to do so as it would involve rewriting a large part of the networking behind Mirror Networking. The client-server model is the modern approach to game networking.

When it comes to choosing the determinism of your game's architecture using Mirror Networking, it's best to go for indeterministic networking. Again, you could build around deterministic principles, but it depends on your needs. We use a client-server, indeterministic model for most use cases.

The client-server model is highly versatile and adaptable to any genre of game, with very few drawbacks.

In the client-server model, we have clients that connect to a game server. First, information gets relayed from the client to the server – then other clients get their information from the server, based on what the server decides the clients should receive.

Let's look at what this model looks like at a conceptual level by looking at Figure 4-4.

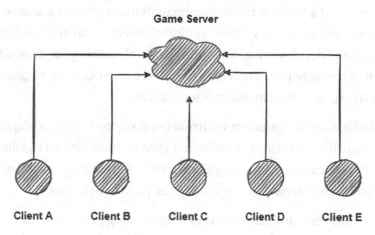

Figure 4-4. *The figure depicts the conceptual architecture of the client-server model*

The client-server model has many benefits, especially when using an authoritative server with a dumb client approach. This authoritative server with a dumb client model approach means that the server has exclusive control over the state of the game, and the dumb clients are simply there for the player to interact with the game server.

Some of these benefits include the following:

- **Difficult to cheat the server** – The authoritative nature of the client-server approach makes it a lot more difficult to cheat than other architectures, especially since you typically host the servers within secure environments.

- **If a client disconnects, other clients are not affected from a networking perspective** – When a client disconnects, the network structure remains the same, meaning that other players can continue as normal. Therefore, from a networking perspective, no other clients are affected. However, in competitive games, this can give one team an advantage over another as the teams will be imbalanced.

- **The architecture is highly scalable** – The client-server architecture is highly performant and scalable. Each node can run over a hundred players with minimal effort, and we can bring additional nodes online to satisfy the player demand.

- **Client performance does not affect the performance of other clients** – Unlike with the lockstep architecture, a client's performance will not affect the performance of the network. The client is simply a listener and a method of interacting with the server for a player and plays no part in how the server functions from an architectural perspective. If a player has incredibly unstable latency, or even if they have low frame performance, the troubled client does not negatively affect the state of the game for other players.

- **Easy to localize the game server to different regions** – We can deploy servers to different regions, allowing our players to connect on a global scale. Players can then interact with players in their region or area with networking not negatively impacting the player experience.

- **Easy to maintain our game servers** – Our hosting providers make it easy to bring servers online or shut them down for maintenance. This flexibility makes maintaining our servers significantly more manageable, and we can often do this with almost no downtime.

- **Our game-servers be deployed to a local network for tournaments in e-sports** – We don't have to host our game servers in the cloud exclusively. Instead, we can deploy our game servers to secure, controller, local networks. This additional flexibility and security are perfect for e-sports tournaments where fairness and zero downtime are critical.

- **Client-server game servers have a singular point of failure** – The client-server model is straightforward on a conceptual level, meaning that if something goes wrong, chances are it's our game server. We can then quickly bring up new servers and diagnose issues with the problematic server.

- **Easy to create failover servers** – If our servers fail, we can create triggers with our hosting providers to load up new servers within seconds and hand our players over to the newly loaded servers, maximizing our service uptime.

- **Extremely easy to reconnect players or hand players over to different game servers** – Should a player disconnect, all they need to do is reconnect to the game server. The state of the game is then easily synchronized across to them. Thus, we can even hand players between different servers with minimal effort, ideal for load balancing.

Understanding the Chain of Command

Now that we understand the different networking architectures and where Mirror Networking falls into it all, we can finally dig deeper into the networking behind our game servers and our clients and finally understand the chain of command.

In Mirror Networking, we use a series of commands and remote procedure calls and state synchronization to represent the client device's server game state representation accurately.

These commands and remote procedure calls may look something like Figure 4-5.

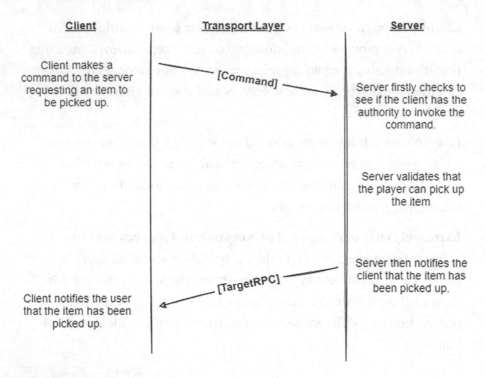

Figure 4-5. *The figure shows an example of how a command and RPC conversation might look like on a conceptual level*

In the preceding example, we have a player that would like to pick up an item. Instead of simply picking up the item, we notify the server and request validation and acknowledgment that the action is permitted. This request validation cycle helps us prevent cheating, but the action then becomes network-bound, meaning that there will be an inherent latency to the action. Latency should be kept in mind when deciding what to make networked. There are also ways to make certain aspects of latency imperceivable by employing client-side prediction techniques. We could, for example, locally allow the player to pick up a copy of the item while we wait for the server's acknowledgment. There are different ways of dealing with client-side prediction. We'll briefly look at these shortly, but first, let's focus on how we can synchronize the game state.

Remote Procedure Calls

Typically, your game will involve several messages between your server and its clients. These messages usually get sent through remote procedure calls, but what exactly are remote procedure calls? Remote procedure calls are an attribute that can be attached to a method, identifying it for Mirror Networking. We can then have the server invoke these remote procedures on our clients. A remote procedure call, a target procedure call, and a command can all use any argument as long as they are of a supported Mirror Networking data type. We covered supported Mirror Networking Data types in the previous chapter. Another key point is that the class calling the RPC, TargetRPC, or Command must inherit from NetworkBehaviour.

The process looks like this (Figure 4-6).

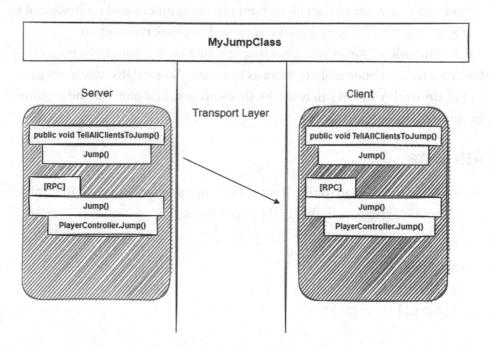

Figure 4-6. *The figure demonstrates how we may use an RPC to make all players jump*

Now, you may notice that both the server and the client have the same logic. That's because in Mirror Networking, we need to remember that the client and the server typically share the same codebase. In the preceding example, the server calls the method "TellAllClientsToJump," which in turn calls the method "Jump."

Jump is tagged with the RPC attribute, identifying it for the Mirror Networking compiler. This tag allows us to pass the method reference through the transport layer, and all clients with the same script attached to the matching network identity will then call the invoked RPC, in this case, the method called "Jump."

Jump then simply calls the local player controller class (just used as an example) and tells the player to jump. Now, making all players jump seems pretty pointless unless you're making some obscure parkour game. So, what if we want to tell a single player to jump?

In this case, we'd use the TargetRPC attribute, which allows us to tell an individual network connection to invoke the associated method. We do this by adding the TargetRPC attribute and giving a NetworkConnection argument as the first argument to the method.

Internally, Mirror Networking will recognize this argument and only attempt to execute the remote procedure call on the specified network connection.

You must include a "NetworkConnection" as the first argument to a target remote procedure call, or your code will not work as intended. Some IDEs may mark the argument as unused. You can safely ignore this warning. The name of the argument also does not matter.

RPC Attribute

Let's take a look at the RPC attribute. If we want to mark a method as an RPC, all we need to do is add the RPC attribute to the method as follows:

```
[RPC]
public void Jump()
{
    PlayerController.Jump();
}
```

It's as simple as that. Now, attaching the script to an object that contains a NetworkIdentity will allow you to call that remote procedure from the server. The remote procedure will execute on all clients that are listening to that network identity; this also includes the host when playing as host. If you'd like to exclude the host from receiving their own RPC call, you can pass a special argument in the attribute flag.

RPC attributes can contain a special argument in the attribute flag called "includeOwner". This defaults to true if you do not pass the argument. If you decide to pass the argument, your new attribute would look more like the following:

```
[RPC(includeOwner = false)]
public void Jump()
{
    PlayerController.Jump();
}
```

And now, your RPC will only execute on clients and exclude the host player. Typically, there aren't many reasons to do this, but the functionality exists.

TargetRPC Attribute

The TargetRPC is much like the RPC attribute. TargetRPC simply stands for Target Remote Procedure Call. Much like the RPC attribute, we need to add an attribute, this time, the TargetRPC attribute.

The TargetRPC requires one additional step, though. We must include a NetworkConnection as an argument to the method as the first argument, or the code will not work. Let's see what that looks like:

```
[TargetRPC]
public void Jump(NetworkConnection connection)
{
    PlayerController.Jump();
}
```

You can then call the remote procedure call and pass in the network connection of the player you would like to invoke the remote procedure on. Some IDEs may warn that the argument is not being used, but this is not the case, and you can safely ignore this warning.

Commands

So, what if we'd like to have a client execute a method on the server? We can use commands to do this; they're much like RPCs, in the sense that we can use command attributes to identify methods for the Mirror Networking compiler.

However, if any client could execute commands on the server, it would make cheating very easy, so there are some requirements in place to make cheating using commands very difficult.

Firstly, the client must have authority over the network identity that it's calling the command on unless overridden by the "ignoreAuthority" argument. Without authority, by default, the server will ignore any commands given and throw out a warning in the console.

Secondly, a command, much like RPCs and TargetRPCs may use any argument as long as they are of a supported Mirror Networking data type.

Lastly, a class containing a command must inherit from NetworkBehaviour.

A command conversation could look something like Figure 4-7.

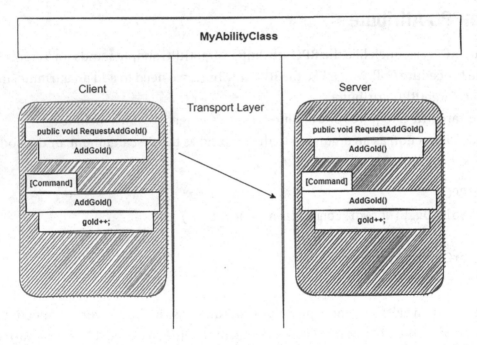

Figure 4-7. *The figure demonstrates how we may use a command to modify a sync-var*

Typically, we use commands to request changes to sync-vars, variables that are synchronized on the network, since only the server may modify the value of the sync-var. We'll discuss these shortly.

Effective networking doesn't just involve RPCs and Commands but instead uses both of them to achieve two-way communication between your clients and the server.

Command Attribute

We can mark a method as a command similar to how we mark methods as RPCs or TargetRPCs. It's important to note that by default, you must have authority over the network identity that you are invoking a command on, which should look something like this:

```
[Command]
public void AddGold()
{
    gold++;
}
```

The given command will allow the client with authority over the network identity to add gold. This gold variable can then be synchronized over the network to other clients through the use of sync-vars, which we'll discuss shortly.

Synchronization – Properties

Synchronization is a Mirror Networking concept where we can synchronize a variable's state over the network. Mirror Networking typically performs this synchronization when a client joins the network or a value changes, and Mirror Networking adds it to the synchronization batch queue.

Synchronization covers two main parts: synchronized properties and synchronization components; the latter are pre-written components that synchronize the state of other components, removing the need to rewrite a lot of boilerplate code from scratch, but are designed to be extended upon to meet the needs of your project.

We'll start off by discussing synchronized properties. These are the following:

- SyncVars
- SyncLists
- SyncDictionaries
- SyncHashSets
- SyncSortedSets

These are versatile properties that allow us to quickly and effectively synchronize our game state, easily connect new or disconnected players, and make cheating more challenging.

Synchronization is incredibly powerful and leverages the indeterministic state-based nature of Mirror Networking. It's also straightforward to get going with, as long as you understand a few principles.

Firstly, only the server may modify a synchronized property, which is an essential note that many beginners struggle with when getting started with Mirror Networking. To change a synchronized value, you must issue a command to the server and have the server modify the property in question. Be sure to make use of supported data types as your arguments when invoking commands.

And secondly, any class using synchronized properties must inherit from NetworkBehaviour.

SyncVars

SyncVars are likely the most used synchronized property that you'll use in Mirror Networking. A sync-var supports any supported data type that Mirror Networking supports. You can even synchronize references to game objects, as long as that game object has an attached network identity and you have spawned the object into the network.

To mark a property as a sync-var, we must add the sync-var attribute to the property. Doing so will look something like this:

```
[SyncVar]
public int gold;
```

Upon marking a property as a sync-var, Unity will serialize the sync-var and show a new kind of property in the inspector, marking it as a sync-var. The new inspector window will look like Figure 4-8.

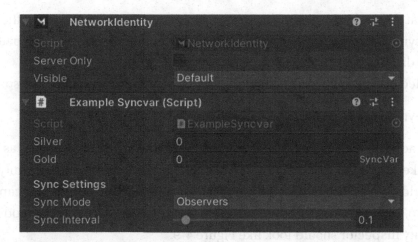

Figure 4-8. *The figure showcases how the unity inspector window serializes sync-var properties*

The figure shows our gold variable marked as a sync-var, and the silver variable is just a standard, nonsynchronized integer.

Once your script has at least one synchronized property, Mirror Networking will extend the inspector to show sync settings. These sync settings are used for batching, which we'll discuss shortly.

Again, it's important to note that only the server can change sync-vars. So, to change a sync-var, the code calling the change needs to be executed on the server. You can do this by using server-side logic or a client with authority over the object calling a command on the server. **One last thing to keep in mind is that a component can only have 64 sync-var properties.**

SyncVars are great, and they're highly efficient. Their values are only replicated over the network when a client's value does not match the sync-var, when a client joins, or when the object becomes visible to the client. We'll discuss network visibility in greater detail in this chapter when we cover interest management.

SyncList

Sync-lists are like sync-vars, but they have a unique type that Mirror Networking can synchronize over the network. Internally, they behave much like the array-based List. Much like sync-vars, they also support any Mirror-supported data type, making it perfect for syncing game state.

The great thing about sync-lists is that Mirror Networking synchronizes them along with other sync-vars on an object, which means that sync-lists benefit from batching, which we'll discuss shortly.

When declaring a sync-list, be sure to initialize it in the declaration, like so:

```
readonly SyncList<Item> items = new SyncList<Item>();
```

We can add the read-only modifier to ensure that the sync-list functions as intended.

Much like sync-vars, sync-lists show differently in the inspector when Unity serializes them and adds sync settings. It's also important to note that only the server can modify sync-lists. So, be sure to use a command to the server when you intend to modify the list.

The Unity inspector should look like Figure 4-9.

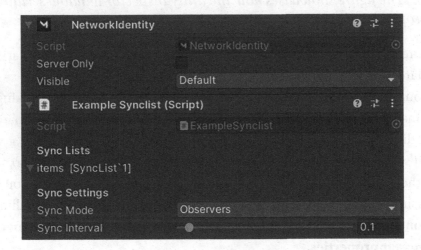

Figure 4-9. *The figure showcases how sync-lists appear in the Unity inspector window when serialized, along with exposing the relevant sync settings*

When working with sync-lists, you should never reassign the list. Making the sync-list read-only helps prevent doing this by accident. Instead, when you should modify the list on the server-side, use the built-in methods.

These built-in methods are as follows:

- **Add** - Adds a new item to the sync-list

- **Clear** - Removes all elements from the list

- **Contains** - Returns a bool that specifies whether or not the item is in the list

- **Flush** - Discards any Mirror queued changes to the sync-list

- **Insert** - Inserts an item into the list at a given index

- **Remove** - Removes the first occurrence of the given item in the list

- **Reset** - Resets the sync object so that we can use it again

- **AddRange** - Adds another collection to this list, appending to it

- **CopyTo** - Copies part or all of the list into an array

- **FindAll** - Retrieves all elements in the list that match a given predicate

- **FindIndex** - Finds an element in the list that matches a given predicate and returns the index of the first occurrence of the element in the list. Returns -1 if it cannot find any element matching the given predicate in the list

- **GetEnumerator** - Returns an enumerator that can iterate through the list

- **IndexOf** - Returns the index of the first occurrence of the given element in the list. Returns -1 if it cannot find an occurrence of the given element in the list

- **InsertRange** - Inserts another collection into this list at the given index

- **RemoveAll** - Removes all elements matching a given predicate

- **RemoveAt** - Removes the element in the list matching the specified index

You can read more about them over at the API documentation by following this URL: `https://mirror-networking.com/docs/api/Mirror.SyncList-1.html`.

Sticking to the provided methods will keep your synchronized state safe when working with sync-lists. You might recognize many of the preceding methods, as they also exist with standard lists. However, you may have also noticed the addition of "Flush" and "Reset."

These methods are Mirror specific and will help significantly.

One last thing to note about sync-lists is that they count toward the 64 sync-var limits on network behavior components. Let's move on to the following type of synchronization property, sync-dictionary.

SyncDictionary

Dictionaries are incredibly fast, unordered arrays that contain key-value pairs, making searching for items extremely efficient and fast. Thankfully, Mirror Networking has not forgotten about these gems. Sync-dictionaries are a dictionary that we can synchronize over the Mirror Network. Internally, sync-dictionaries are dotNet dictionaries, and it's good to keep that in mind as they share much of the same functionality.

An excellent advantage that sync-dictionaries have is that much like the sync-list, we only synchronize changes over the network, and it takes advantage of Mirror's sync-var batching. We can also use any data type supported by Mirror Networking.

Adding a sync-dictionary to your network behavior is also straightforward. Much like the sync-list, it is a type, so we do not need to use attributes for this. You must also initialize the dictionary during its declaration. Your code might look something like this:

```
public readonly SyncDictionary<string, int> itemSaleValues = new
SyncDictionary<string, int>();
```

We typically declare the sync-dictionary as read-only to prevent accidental reassignment of the dictionary. The dictionary may only be altered, not reassigned.

We can access the keys by accessing the property, "Keys." And similarly, we can access values by accessing the property, "Values."

Additionally, we can also access the dictionary by the indexer, like in the following example:

```
Debug.Log(itemSaleValues["Diamond Sword"]);
```

Accessing a key that does not exist yet will, however, return a KeyNotFound exception. You can consider using TryGetValue, which is significantly more efficient if you're unsure whether or not the key exists within your dictionary. Your code may look something like this:

```
itemSaleValues.TryGetValue("Diamond Sword", out var value);
Debug.Log(value);
```

Another great thing about using accessors is that you can easily set keys by simply assigning them to the accessor:

```
itemSaleValues["Diamond Sword"] = 100;
```

If the key does not exist, it will add a new entry to the dictionary, and if one already exists, it will overwrite the entry.

Mirror Networking also provides custom Unity serialization in the inspector window for sync-dictionaries. Let's take a look at Figure 4-10.

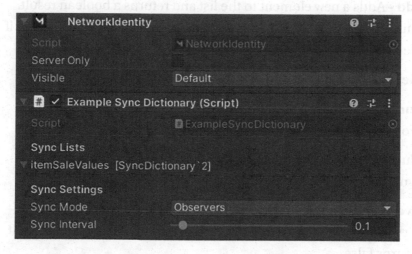

Figure 4-10. *The figure showcases how sync-dictionaries appear similarly to sync-lists in the Unity inspector window when serialized, along with exposing the relevant sync settings*

Overall, sync-dictionaries are an incredible asset to creating scalable multiplayer solutions in Unity.

SyncHashSet

Finally, we have the SyncHashSet. SyncHashSets are Mirror Networking implementations of C# hashsets from Microsoft. Hashsets are essentially really fast dictionaries with no value pairs. This high performance makes them an ideal tool for large-scale networking.

Much like the sync-list and sync-dictionary, they have their type, and you should initialize them during declaration. I would also advise adding the "readonly" keyword to ensure against accidentally reallocating the SyncHashSet.

Your declaration code could look something like this, bearing in mind that the class should inherit from Network Behavior:

```
public readonly SyncHashSet<string> modifiers = new SyncHashSet<string>();
```

Much like SyncLists, SyncHashSets have a few ways that we can modify their values, which should always be done from the server. However, SyncHashSets are exceptionally good at performing set operations and contain no duplication. Let's take a look at a few of these:

- **Add** - Adds a new element to the list and returns a boolean result. This result is true if the operation was successful and returns false if the element already exists.

- **Clear** - Clears the set and sets the capacity to zero.

- **Contains** - The SyncHashSet returns a boolean value stating if the provided element exists in the set or not.

- **Flush** - Discards any queued Mirror Networking changes to the SyncHashSet.

- **Overlaps** - Compares this SyncHashSet with another collection; if they share at least one element, then this returns true; otherwise, it returns false.

- **Remove** - Removes an element from the SyncHashSet, returns true if the operation was successful, or returns false if the element could not be found.

- **Reset** - Resets the SyncHashSet so it can be reused by Mirror Networking.

- **CopyTo** - Copies the elements of the SyncHashSet into an array.

- **ExceptWith** - Removes all elements from the SyncHashSet that are present in a given collection.

- **IntersectWith** - Modifies the current SyncHashSet so that it only contains elements that were present within its own collection and a given collection.

- **SetEquals** - Determine if the SyncHashSet and a given collection are completely identical and return true if they are or false if they are not.

- **UnionWith** - Merges this SyncHashSet with a given collection.

- **IsSubsetOf** - Determines if the SyncHashSet is a subset of a given collection.

- **IsSupersetOf** - Determines if the SyncHashSet is a superset of a given collection.

- **SymmetricExceptionWith** - The SyncHashSet is modified to only include elements that were in the SyncHashSet or a given collection but not in both.

- **LinqMethods** - The SyncHashSet also supports Linq methods, which are extremely useful when working with collections.

SyncHashSets are fast, and they're great! They really help with creating massive, scalable architecture. As with before, you can find more details on these methods by following the Mirror Networking API documentation.

Let's take a look into how synchronized variables shine, batching.

Batching

Batching is a functionality of Mirror Networking that helps it shine when it comes to large-scale multiplayer. Mirror Networking batches any sync-var changes made to network behavior and sends them all in the same message over the network.

This batching functionality significantly reduces TCP and UDP packet header overhead and helps us achieve that holy grail of MMO scale networking.

When you add a sync-var to network behavior, any changes that we make to the variable will get added to a queue – and they are all included in the same network message.

When doing this, as you will have noticed by now, we see some new options available to us in the inspector window of our component, the sync settings. These sync settings help us control how our network behavior should batch changes.

Firstly, we have the sync mode, from which we have two options to choose from, they are

- Observers

- Owner

These options give us even more flexibility when it comes to synchronized variables.

Setting the mode to Observers, the default value, will synchronize the data to all observers of the networked object. Thus, observer mode is beneficial for variables that need to be accessed by other players, not just an individual player.

And then there is the Owner mode. The Owner mode will tell the server only to synchronize the data between itself and the client with authority over the network identity.

Being mindful of the synchronization mode can help you reduce network bandwidth and save on some performance.

Next, we have the sync interval. This synchronization interval is the interval measured in seconds between batch updates.

So, suppose you have a sync interval of one. In that case, your variable will be synchronized between players once per second. Any changes that occur to the variable between that interval will be batched together into the same message.

So, what if we don't want to use batching, in say, a high-priority variable? In that case, we can set the sync interval to zero. Setting the batch interval to zero will disable the batching on the network behavior component and synchronize changes between players as they happen.

SyncVar Hooks

So, what do we do if we want to know that a value has changed? Could we take a classic approach of storing the previous values and checking against them? Unfortunately, though, this adds additional development time and isn't suitable for performance. So, instead, we can use something provided by Mirror Networking called sync-var hooks.

Sync-var hooks are a powerful and elegant solution to detecting when the network updates the variables of our clients. They allow us to "hook" into the variable, which notifies us whenever that variable changes, and act upon it by invoking a method.

To use SyncVar Hooks, you'll need to use the SyncVar attribute with an additional step. Your updated SyncVar attribute should look something like the following:

```
[SyncVar(hook = nameof(UpdateScoreText))]
private int score = 0;

public TMP_Text scoreText;
```

```
public void UpdateScoreText(int oldValue, int newValue)
{
    scoreText.text = $"Score: {newValue}";
}
```

So here, we add a SyncVar with an added argument. The "nameof" method points to the method that we'd like to execute whenever we set the associated property or if the network synchronization sets the property. However, it's important to note that changing the inspector's value will not trigger SyncVarHook.

The method you target with a SyncVarHook must contain two arguments of the same type as your SyncVar. We get the first value as the old value and the latter as the new value. You can use these however you see fit, and the name of the arguments does not matter.

In the previous example, whenever the score int property is set (via code or set via the SyncVar), it will invoke the UpdateScoreText. Thus, we don't need to check for changes to the score in every frame. Instead, we only execute the code when required.

With that knowledge at your disposal, you'll be able to build incredibly scalable and efficient games. So, let's move on to the following type of synchronization, components.

Synchronization – Components

Synchronization or network components are simply pre-written components designed to synchronize common functions over the network. They're helpful, save you a lot of time, and Mirror Networking has designed these to be extensible as a bonus.

Several synchronization components come with Mirror Networking:

- NetworkAnimator

- NetworkLerpRigidbody

- NetworkRigidbody (2D and 3D Variants)

- NetworkTransform

- NetworkTransformChild

- Some experimental components

I'm encouraging you to open these components and look at how they function internally. There's a lot of extra information to be learned there. First, however, I will discuss each of these components. Then, let's dig into their purpose, what the properties do, and how to use them.

The most common synchronization component that you'll likely use is the Network Transform component.

Network Transform

The Network Transform component allows you to replicate the transform of the attached game object. The component will require you to attach a network identity to the game object in question.

The network transform looks something like Figure 4-11.

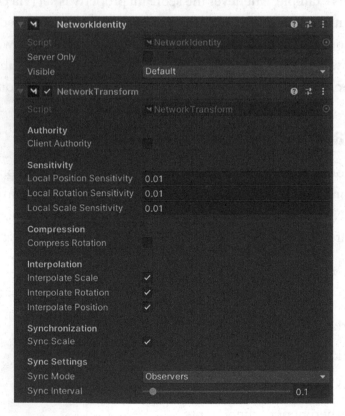

Figure 4-11. *The figure shows the Network Transform inspector window within Unity*

So, firstly, we have the client authority checkbox. This boolean value decides who controls the Network Transform. By default, the checkbox is disabled, meaning that only the server may move the given object.

Having the server control the object is great in most situations, but what about when you want the player to move the object? In that case, the player should have authority over the object, such as an object spawned for the given player or the player object.

After the player has authority over the network identity, you'll want to ensure that the client authority checkbox is enabled. Now, whenever the client with authority moves the game object, such as with "Transform.SetPositionAndRotation," then the game object's transform values will be replicated to the server and back to all other clients.

Adding network movement to your game is as simple as that!

Next, there are the sensitivity options. These determine how much of a change we need to make to the transform's values to trigger a synchronization. There's no point in synchronizing an object that's not moving.

Then, we have the compression settings. These settings allow us to compress the rotation of the transform. Compressing rotations can save some bandwidth, resulting in slightly less accurate rotations or some minor weird behavior in some situations. If you don't need a rotation to be perfect and you need the extra bandwidth, you can look to this setting.

Then, you have interpolation settings. For example, synchronizing scale every 0.1 seconds would look choppy. That's where the interpolation comes in. You can use interpolation to fill in the blanks between synchronizations, resulting in smoother movement.

Then, there's the option of synchronizing scale. This option is there because sometimes, we may not need to synchronize the scale, such as in situations where the scale should always remain the same. In cases like these, you can simply disable scale synchronization to save on some bandwidth.

So, if NetworkTransforms require a network identity, you may have noticed an issue.

What happens if you need a network transform to be the child of network identity. As you know, network identities cannot be a child of another network identity. So, how do we get around this?

The answer is the Network Transform Child component. Let's take a look.

Network Transform Child

The Network Transform Child serves the same purpose as the network transform component, in that its goal is to synchronize the transform of a game object. In addition, however, Network Transform Children can target child game objects of the network identity.

You still attach the network transform child to the network identity, and you can have as many as needed, though I'd urge you to keep performance and bandwidth in mind. But instead of just attaching it to the network identity, you assign a target.

The Network Transform Child component is identical to the Network Transform component, with the additional field labeled "target."

Network Animator

The network animator is an extraordinary component that is excellent for expanding upon. Out of the box, it can synchronize animation states for a given animator within the child hierarchy of the associated network identity (Figure 4-12).

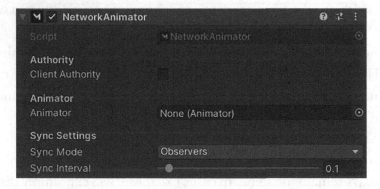

Figure 4-12. *The figure shows the network animator within the inspector window of Unity*

The network animator has a boolean checkbox that we're pretty familiar with by this point, the client authority checkbox. This boolean value determines whether or not the server should control the animation state or if a client with authority should modify the animation state.

The network animator also has a reference to an animator. This animator reference should point to your animator. The animator can either be on the network identity or as a child of the network identity.

Then finally, we have the usual sync settings.

Network Lerp Rigidbody

The Network Lerp Rigidbody component is an alternative to managing transform replication. It's advantageous in a situation where you want to replicate a non-kinematic rigid body over the network.

However, using a Network Transform on a rigid body may yield odd behavior with the physics system, as the rigid body itself will not have its velocity modified. To counteract this issue, we have the Network Lerp Rigidbody.

A Network Lerp Rigidbody synchronizes the velocity values of the rigid body and its associated position.

It's important to note that a network identity should not have a Network Transform and a Network Lerp Rigidbody component. You should choose one or the other depending on the needs of your product, typically favoring Network Transform, unless velocity is important – such as rigidbody platforms, or player interactable rigidbodies. Let's take a look at the component in Figure 4-13.

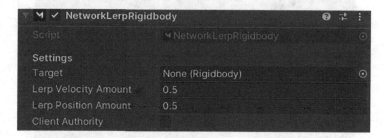

Figure 4-13. *The figure shows the Network Lerp Rigidbody component*

Much like the Network Transform Child, we have a target, the associated rigidbody, we want to have replicated. Then, there are our lerp settings. These lerp settings dictate how much the component should attempt to fill in the blanks between network synchronization ticks.

Finally, we have the client authority boolean value that we've become familiar with, which determined who has permission to control the networked rigid body.

Network Rigidbody (2D and 3D Variants)

The Network Rigidbody is another method of synchronizing rigidbodies over the network. However, these do not interpolate their values. There are Network Rigidbody components for both 2D and 3D rigidbodies.

Its synchronization properties are a bit different from the Network Lerp Rigidbody component (Figure 4-14) that we just covered, so let's look at it.

Here, we also have a target that we can specify. We also have the addition of some checkboxes that give us more control over what properties should be synchronized.

This additional control can help us reduce network bandwidth in many situations where we might only want to synchronize velocity, such as a moving platform that does not rotate.

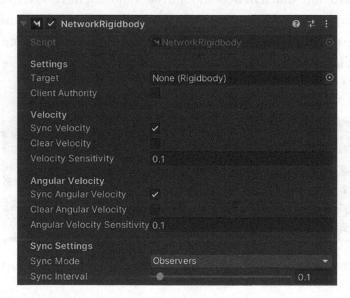

Figure 4-14. *The figure shows the Network Lerp Rigidbody component*

Network Messages

So, what if you're looking for a little more control than RPCs and Commands? There are other ways of having the server communicate with its clients and vice versa. These are called Network Messages, and you're not required to use game objects.

While RPCs and Commands are ideal in most situations, network messages open up an additional way of developing aspects of your game that might be tricky to do otherwise. You can use network messages if you'd like to work on a lower level of Mirror Networking by implementing the NetworkMessage interface into your structs and then pass those over the network.

Ideally, you should only use Network Messages where necessary as you can achieve most of the needed functionality with the previously mentioned RPCs and Commands. Let's take a look at how we can implement these network messages, though.

This process requires a few steps:

1. We need to create a struct containing the data that we'd like to send and receive.

2. The struct should then implement the NetworkMessage interface.

3. You need to register the handler with the NetworkClient class and create a method with your logic that you'd like to send the message to.

4. Then, you need to send the data.

Let's take a look at these steps in more detail.

Creating the Struct Containing Our Data

The struct should contain data that we need, and this data needs to be of a supported Mirror Networking data type that we discussed in the previous chapter. I'll create an example where we create a chat system for players, though we can use Network Message for just about anything.

So, let's do this in the following example:

```
public struct ChatMessage
{
    public string playerName;
    public string playerMessage;
}
```

Firstly, I'd point out that I'd avoid taking this approach for a chat service since players could easily forge messages using this system. The purpose here is simply to convey how we can use NetworkMessage.

We first declare the struct like in the given example, then we can move on to the next step.

Have the Struct Implement the Network Message Interface

Next, we need to ensure that the struct is implementing the Network Message interface:

```
public struct ChatMessage : NetworkMessage
{
    public string playerName;
    public string playerMessage;
}
```

It's as simple as that; now, let's move on to the next step.

You Need to Register the Handler with the NetworkClient Class and Create a Method to Handle the Data

In order to actually know when we receive a Network Message and, more importantly, what to do with it, we need to register a callback with the NetworkClient class.

This process is really straightforward, and you can generally do this during the Start method. It's important to note that this should be called before you receive the network message, or you won't have any logic that executes once the NetworkClient receives the Network Message.

Let's go ahead and do that:

```
private void Start()
{
    NetworkClient.RegisterHandler<ChatMessage>(ReceiveNewChatMsg);
}
```

Great! So, what this line of code is doing is telling the network client that when it receives a message of type ChatMessage, then pass it through to ReceiveNewChatMsg. Now, of course, we haven't created the ReceiveNewChatMsg method yet, so let's do that:

```
public void ReceiveNewChatMsg(ChatMessage message)
{
```

```
Debug.Log($"{message.playerName}: {message.playerMessage}\n");
}
```

What this method does is it takes the ChatMessage object received from the Network Client and then displays a debug message, with the player's name and their message.

Perfect! Now, one final step we need to perform is to actually send a Network Message.

Sending a NetworkMessage of type ChatMessage

Sending the NetworkMessage is also really straightforward! All we need to do is create a new ChatMessage object, fill out the properties, and send it to the Network Server to be sent across the network.

Let's take a look at how this is done:

```
public void SendTestMessage()
{
    ChatMessage message = new ChatMessage()
    {
        playerName = "John Doe",
        playerMessage = "Hello World!"
    };

    // Send from server to all clients, even clients that are not fully
    // connected
    // yet.
    NetworkServer.SendToAll(message);

    // Send from client to server.
    NetworkClient.Send(message);

    // Send to a specific connection.
    // Get a reference to the connection, like using a network identity of the
    // connection.
    targetPlayer.networkIdentity.Send(message);

    // We can also send messages to only clients that are ready by calling this.
    NetworkServer.SendToReady();
}
```

That's how you handle network messages in Mirror Networking. The whole process is straightforward. Again, I would like to mention that RPC and Command will generally be your go-to for communicating between clients and the server. However, Network Message is excellent for message exchanges between clients who are still connecting and authenticating.

Client-Side Prediction

Client-side prediction minimizes the impact of latency to reduce the effect that authoritative controls have on the player. Mirror Networking itself has no built-in solutions for client-side prediction, but there are a few techniques that we can use to minimize the impact of latency.

Let's take a look at some of these methods:

- Give players authority over their player objects or objects that they are responsible for on the network.

- Create a player simulator that runs only on the server that interprets the player's input and corrects the actual player's position if that value deviated too far.

- Value check and sanitize player commands and inputs.

Now, we need to remember the golden rule of game network programming. Never trust the player. There will be cheaters.

With that said, the majority of the traffic you receive will be valid traffic. So, you must choose a client-side prediction technique that matches your project's effort requirements and budget. Spending the majority of time reducing the impact of cheating on a local-co-op game might not be the best focus of development resources, whereas if you're developing a competitive title, then investing time into developing advanced techniques would be more worthwhile.

Give Players Authority Over Their Player Objects

Giving players authority over their player objects is the standard practice for Mirror Networking. The player will have control over their player and its position. This approach works in a large majority of situations and requires no additional effort on your part. If you are concerned about cheating, then it would be beneficial to look at an anti-cheat provider. Since the player controls their object, it's not reliant on waiting for the server to echo its position back.

Because the player is not reliant on waiting for the server to echo its position back, there is no perception of latency in player movement input.

Create a Sanitized Player Server-Side Simulation

This approach would require additional work but is an approach that you could take. In this approach, you create a sanitized server-side copy of the player and mimic the player's inputs. If the player deviates too far from the clone, you instruct the player to correct its position, rotation, or other values. If the client ignores the correction attempt, then you can simply disconnect the player.

This approach is not viable for every kind of game, and you will have to determine if your game's structure is deterministic enough for this approach.

Value Check and Sanitize Player Commands and Inputs

This approach, combined with giving players authority over their player objects, is excellent. With this approach, we can minimize the impact of network latency and detect cheating clients.

This approach aims to detect any values that are out of the ordinary and flag those clients as potentially malicious. You can send the correct values back to the client for correction, and if the values are not corrected, you can disconnect the client and flag it for further action.

Spawning

Instantiating objects during runtime is a vital requirement for almost any game. Thankfully, instantiating objects over the network is not only possible with Mirror Networking, but it's also straightforward. There are some things you should know first, though.

To instantiate an object on the network, you need to be doing this from the server. The server has the authority to create a new game object on the network and replicate that information to the connected clients. To instantiate a game object on the network, you need to first instantiate the prefab locally on the server. Once that happens, you can then spawn the object onto the network.

The act of spawning begins replicating that game object over the network. There are five requirements to this:

- **You need to instantiate the prefab locally on the server initially** -
  You can instantiate the object locally by calling the "GameObject.
  Instantiate" method.

- **You must spawn a prefab that the client knows how to access** - For
  example, the client needs to access the prefab file with the matching
  asset id.

- **You must register the prefab with the Network Manager** - You
  can find this in the currently active Network Manager's "Spawnable
  Prefabs" list. There are also ways to register the prefab during
  runtime. We'll discuss this shortly.

- **You must call the spawning command from the server** - Only the
  server may spawn an object onto the network.

- **The registered prefab must have a network identity component** -
  This network identity component should exist in the prefab root. You
  cannot register a spawnable prefab without a network identity.

In Mirror Networking, we use the term "Spawn" to indicate an object becoming
active on the network.

Spawning objects is excellent because it allows new clients to connect and
immediately be aware of the spawned object and its current state.

At a conceptual level, the lifecycle of a spawned object looks something Figure 4-15.

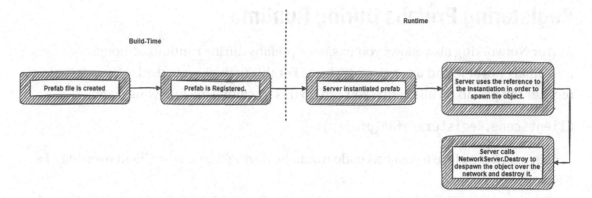

Figure 4-15. *The figure shows the conceptual lifecycle of a networked game object*

Let's take a look at a code example of how this could work. Firstly, create a game object with a network identity, and make it a prefab. Delete the prefab from the scene, and add a reference to the network manager's spawnable prefabs list.

Then create a new network behavior, and add the following code:

```
public GameObject spawnPrefab;
private GameObject _testObjectReference;

public void SpawnTestPrefab()
{
    _testObjectReference = Instantiate(spawnPrefab);
    NetworkServer.Spawn(_testObjectReference);
}
```

In the given code, calling "SpawnTestPrefab" will instantiate a copy of the prefab. We then store a reference to that prefab and finally call "NetworkServer.Spawn" using that reference as an argument.

Destroying network objects is slightly different from destroying standard game objects. Instead of calling "GameObject.Destroy", we need to call "NetworkServer. Destory". We are using "NetworkServer.Destroy" to safely despawn and destroy the game object across the network for both the server and all connected clients.

Registering Prefabs During Runtime

Mirror Networking also allows you to spawn prefabs during runtime, although I've personally never found any reason to do so. For this to work, you need to ensure that you register the prefab on all clients. You can do this by calling the following code:

```
ClientScene.RegisterPrefab(prefab);
```

An excellent place to call this code would be during the OnStartClient override of a Network Behavior.

Registering prefabs during runtime doesn't offer much benefit since the registered prefab must share the same ID across all clients. There is also the fact that prefabs cannot be created during runtime removing many use cases.

For the most part, I'd just recommend ensuring that you register any prefab that you intend to spawn with the network manager.

Mirror's Order of Events

Much like Unity, which has Awake, Start, OnTriggerEnter, and many others, Mirror Networking also has events. These events get invoked throughout the lifecycle of a Mirror Networking instance.

The events occur in the following order:

- Awake (Unity)
- OnStartServer
- OnRebuildObservers
- OnStartAuthority
- OnStartClient
- OnSetHostVisibility
- OnStartLocalPlayer
- Start (Unity)

You can access these methods by overriding the method within any Network Behavior. Let's take a look at each of these events and see where we might use them.

OnStartServer

OnStartServer is called on a network behavior when it becomes active on the server. OnStartServer is only ever called on the server and can be helpful in initial server-side setup, such as initializing variables. It is the first Networking callback called on a Network Behavior.

OnStartAuthority

The network behavior invokes this callback on the client when the client gains authority over the network behavior. This invocation happens for player objects and when the server grants authority to the given player. It is only called on clients as the server always has authority over game objects.

OnStartClient

OnStartClient is only called on clients. The network behavior invokes this callback when it spawns the network object on the local client.

OnStartLocalPlayer

"OnStartLocalPlayer" is called when the server spawns the local player's object. The network behavior invokes this callback after "OnStartAuthority" and "OnStartClient."

Start

Finally, after all of the given callbacks happen, we get the standard Unity "Start" callback.

Interest Management

Having hundreds of players connected to a game session is made possible by Mirror Networking, but that's not to say that all of your clients will be able to handle that many active players at once. There's a lot of processing involved in player objects, from physics to rendering to general game logic. As such, in most cases, you'll want to limit how many players a player can see to those in the immediate vicinity. Or, if you're developing a competitive title, you may want to curb cheating by not revealing the locations of all players within a game map.

Mirror Networking is excellent at handling use cases like those previously mentioned using a concept called interest management. It's so good at this that there's almost no reason not to use it.

There are three approaches you can take when it comes to interest management. I'll cover the first two in more detail, as creating a completely custom solution is out of the scope of this book. "If it ain't broken, don't fix it."

These approaches are the following:

- Using a ready-built system from Mirror Networking

- Expanding the system that Mirror Networking provides

- Creating a custom solution

Mirror Networking provides two out-of-the-box solutions to interest management that just work. There is also a legacy interest management class that I would advise against using.

Let's take a look at these.

Distance Interest Management

Distance interest management is the traditional approach to handling interest management. With this approach, we add a distance interest management component to our network manager game object. That's it, congratulations! You've successfully implemented distance-based interest management. Yes, it's that easy.

Let's take a look at the component,

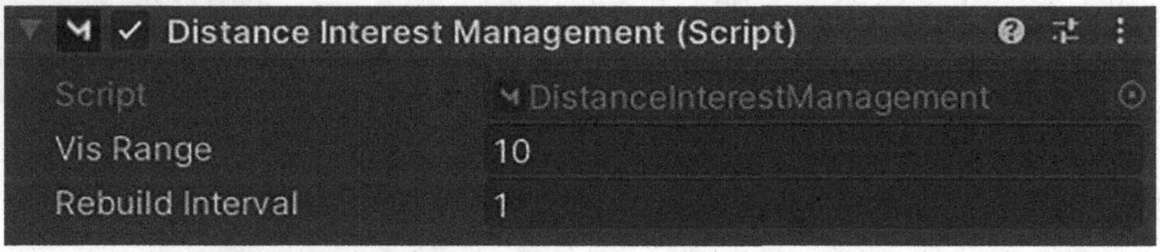

Figure 4-16. The figure shows the distance interest management component

The component has two properties available to us (Figure 4-16).

- **Vis Range** - This is our visibility range. The visibility range determines the range at which connections can receive state updates about objects in the world.

- **Rebuild Interval** - This is a time in seconds in which the distance checks occur.

The distance-based interest management is a great starter template, and I'd highly recommend digging into the code to see how it works. You can expand upon this class just like with the many other Mirror Networking classes out there.

So, is distance-based interest management the best solution to interest management?

Well, no. The thing about distance-based interest management is that it doesn't scale very well. Each player is running distance checks against every other player.

Let's take a look at Figure 4-17.

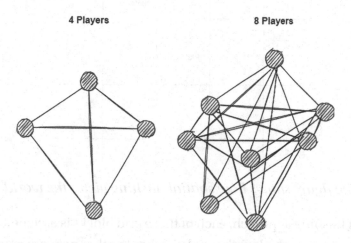

4 Players   **8 Players**

Figure 4-17.   *The figure shows how poorly distance-based interest management scales*

As you can see, adding just a few more players already makes things messy. This poor scaling significantly impairs performance. (Trust me, just drawing that diagram was a nightmare.)

So, if distance-based interest management has poor scaling, then what other options are there? The scalable solution that I'd recommend is spatial hashing. Let's talk a bit about spatial hashing.

Spatial Hashing-Based Interest Management

Spatial hashing is an industry term that sounds intimidating, but it is actually really straightforward, and implementing it is even easier. Instead of checking the distance between each connection, we split the world into a grid (Figure 4-18). From this grid, we share the neighbor grids to determine which connections are within range to receive state updates.

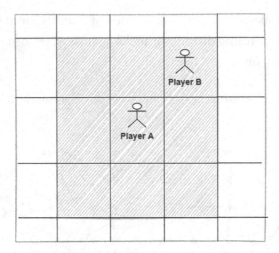

Figure 4-18. *The figure shows how spatial hashing views the world*

In the spatial hashing approach, each of these grid blocks is assigned a hash. Then, the server can compare each player's visible hashes to other network entities in the scene and determine what states should be synchronized.

Implementing spatial hashing is insanely straightforward; simply attach a spatial hashing interest management component to your network manager game object, and you're good to go.

Let's take a look at the properties exposed to us.

Figure 4-19. *The figure showcases the spatial hashing interest management component in the Unity inspector window*

The spatial hashing component exposes four properties for us to play with (Figure 4-19):

- **Vis range** - The visibility range that state updates should occur at.

- **Rebuild interval** - The rebuild interval in seconds, which determines how often we should check for grid positional changes.

- **Check method** - The check method determines if the grid is on the XZ or XY plane. Change this depending on the style of your game.

- **Show slider** - Toggles a debug slider that you can tweak.

Once you've added the spatial hashing interest management component and tweaked the properties, you're good to go. Congratulations, you now have scalable interest management within your game.

A Note About Hosts

Clients running in host mode can toggle interest management by calling the following code:

```
NetworkIdentity.SetHostVisibility(bool)
```

And that covers it for interest management. There are many custom implementations that you can build, and I'd encourage reading into the Mirror Networking documentation for more on this.

Creating Our First Multiplayer Game

I have a challenge for you. Using the knowledge that you've acquired so far, I'd like you to build a small game. The goal of the game is to reach a given score while playing against other players. We'll be looking to create a game inspired by Agar.io and Snake.io

Your game should have the following:

- An offline scene (the menu)

- An online scene (the game world)

The player should spawn at a random location within the game world at a given starting size. The player starts at 10 points. As the player moves around the map, they should be able to pick up pieces of food that spawn throughout the map.

Each food piece is worth 1 point, and the player increases by a size increment every 10 points. If the player collides with an opposing player that is smaller than them, the opposing player is eaten, and the points are transferred to the player.

If the player is eaten by an opposing player, then they respawn randomly on the map with their starting 10 points and their original points are transferred to the opposing player.

The game should also have an exit menu, as well as the option to return to the main menu.

What If I Get Stuck?

To help you with this challenge, I've created a sample game based on the iconic snake.io game. I encourage you to tear apart the code and learn from it to beat the challenge that I've provided.

You can access the GitHub repository for the sample using the following link.

`https://github.com/VoidFletcher/MirrorSamples-WormGame`

Please feel free to reach out with any issues or questions via GitHub issue tracking.

CHAPTER 5

The Memory of a Goldfish

So far, we've covered how to create multiplayer games in Unity using Mirror Networking, but that's only a part of the battle when creating large, scalable multiplayer products. In the following chapters, I'll discuss how we can implement data persistence for our users and deploy our games in a scalable manner.

In this chapter, I'll primarily focus on data persistence, so let's dig right in.

What Is Data Persistence, and Why Is It Important?

When we talk about data persistence in games, we're referring to persisting the user's efforts between play sessions. You can typically achieve this in single-player games by saving and loading from a file using various techniques, from JSON files to serialized binary files. However, these techniques often fall short when dealing with large-scale multiplayer where the server is responsible for loading the save states for thousands, if not hundreds of thousands of players. The techniques fall short due to the efficiency of accessing these datasets as they grow.

I'll discuss how to approach data persistence for smaller, co-op games where your game servers won't be strained by loading from a typical file. Once done with that, I'll discuss how to implement database storage for large-scale games.

Data Persistence Using Player Prefs

The traditional approach to saving and loading uses Unity's "PlayerPrefs" class to read and write to a platform-specific location. Utilizing this approach is similar to working with a dictionary because you use a key to set or retrieve an associated value.

Unity will read and write to a file instead of accessing the data in memory.

© Dylan Engelbrecht 2022
D. Engelbrecht, *Building Multiplayer Games in Unity*, https://doi.org/10.1007/978-1-4842-7474-3_5

Pros of Using Player Prefs for Data Persistence:

- **Simple to use** - Using player prefs is almost as easy as using a standard C# dictionary.

- **Supports all platforms** - Player prefs is designed with different platforms in mind, even WebGL.

- **Unlimited keys** - Player prefs writes game save data to binary and theoretically supports unlimited keys, except WebGL, limiting the file to 1Mb.

Cons of Using Player Prefs for Data Persistence

- **Player prefs is slow** - One of the biggest downfalls of player prefs is speed. Player prefs lacks the performance needed for large, scalable games. For small, co-op games, or single-player games, the amount of data required would likely not be enough to be noticeable from a performance standpoint. However, if you plan to build large, scalable games, player prefs is not a viable option.

- **Lack of security for accounts** - Player prefs are not a good way of handling user accounts. The data is not encrypted, and the effects of a data breach would be catastrophic.

- **Not scalable** - Player prefs is not suitable as a database for large, scalable multiplayer games. It doesn't have any support for synchronizing over multiple server locations.

As we can see, player prefs is a powerful tool for small games that need minimal data persistence. However, it falls short for large, scalable multiplayer games. So, I'd encourage you to use it if you're starting with multiplayer development or developing a local co-op game. Still, if you begin to move onto dedicated servers, it would be wise to look elsewhere for your data persistence needs.

So, if player prefs are not suitable for scalable multiplayer games, then what is?

Data Persistence for Large-Scale Multiplayer Games

When it comes to global, scalable games, the best choice of data persistence is using databases. Databases are widely available and are a highly performant way of handling user data securely. We can even have multiple game servers served by a single database.

Pros of Using a Database for Data Persistence

- **Highly performant** - Developers have created databases with performance in mind. Almost all websites and applications that you use interact with a database at some point in its lifecycle.

- **Scalable** - Speed and scalability are at the heart of database design. Whether you're serving a thousand users or a billion users, databases are designed for scalability.

- **Affordable** - Hosting a database is easy to do on your own, and there are many inexpensive services out there that can do it for you.

- **Secure** - Very importantly, when it comes to databases, security is a core focus.

Cons of Using a Database for Data Persistence

- **Can be challenging at first** - Databases can be challenging at first, but they start to make sense quickly. However, it can take years to master database development, maintenance, and administration.

- **Requires a bit of extra development time** - You'll need to design and implement your database architecture and program the interface between your database and your game server. This additional work can add development time into the mix.

So, what exactly are databases?

What Are Database Engines?

The chances are that you've heard the term database before, but what exactly is a database, and what on earth is a database engine? A database is a structured set of data that conforms to the rules of its database engine. Typically, databases contain a primary key that we use to access data within a table. One can think of a primary key like our main search property, like a file name, and the table being the folder that we'd like to search in; however, the power of databases shines because we can search by various parameters in a highly performant manner.

On the other hand, a database engine is what we use to perform those searches and store our database within. Typically, we connect to the database engine and execute queries to interact with our database. Think of it as our gatekeeper. The database engine ensures that we have the correct authorization to access specific tables, enforce security policies, manage backups, and monitor the performance of our database.

From a programming perspective, you can view databases almost like a collection of dictionaries, but it's important to note a difference between the two.

Another critical concept to understand is that not all databases follow the same structure. The most significant structural difference between database engines is that some are relational and some are not. Let's go into more detail about relational and non-relational databases.

Relational vs. Non-relational Databases

Let's start with relational databases. Relational databases consist of tables, each with a fixed number of columns. These are the spreadsheet-esque tables that make up traditional databases. Each column supports a specific data type configured when designing the database. What makes relational databases so powerful is that each column can refer to another table's data using relationships.

For example, if we have a player's kill table containing a list of all killed players, we can use a key for each player, then retrieve information about that key, such as the player's name, from the user's table. Let's take a look at that example in Figure 5-1.

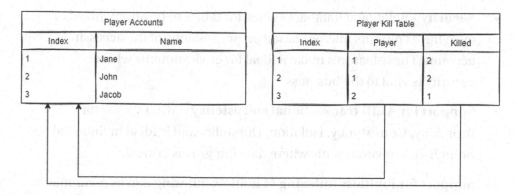

Figure 5-1. *The figure shows how a player's kill list would look in a relational database*

With relational databases, we don't ever store duplicate data. The player kill table in the preceding example contains references to the index of player accounts. Using the index is not always the best approach, but it suits the purpose of the preceding model.

By having these relationships, we're able to build our results with a SQL query. If you're going to be fulfilling a database development role in your career, I would highly recommend taking a short course in SQL to get a more in-depth understanding of the language. However, we will cover it at a surface level later in this chapter.

The results of a SQL query on the recent model could look something like Figure 5-2.

Player Kills		
Index	Player	Killed
1	Jane	John
2	Jane	John
3	John	Jane

Figure 5-2. *The figure shows how a query result could look like using Figure 5-1's kill table*

Using relational databases allows us to prevent duplicate data when used correctly and allows us some flexibility. We can, for example, change John's name to Eric without losing any data within the player kill table.

Let's take a look at the pros and cons of relational databases.

Pros of Relational Databases

- **Security** - Relational databases allow for tables to be anonymized or even have columns masked based on permissions of the accessing account. These features make it ideal for environments where security is vital to the business.

- **Support for ACID transactional consistency** - ACID stands for Atomicity, Consistency, Isolation, Durability and is ideal in financial or high-risk environments where data integrity is critical.

- **Support for limitless indexing** - Limitless indexing makes relational databases ideal for transactional data, data warehousing, CRM, and ERP systems.

- **Relationship constraints** - Fields must always conform to the given tables. These constraints make the data rigid and can be suitable for ensuring consistent data. It is great for enterprise environments.

- **Matured** - Relational databases have been around for a long, long time, and as such, the technology has matured with plenty of support available.

Cons of Relational Databases

- **Difficult to scale and expand upon an already-existing database** - Relational databases are a pain to scale horizontally. Adding new tables and columns to an in-production database can be a nightmare even for an experienced database developer.

- **Inadequate for handling varied data** - Relational databases require consistency and rigidity in the data that they process.

Relational databases are powerful, but they're not always the best answer to your database needs. Typically, relational databases are ideal in enterprise environments. Let's see what the alternative, non-relational databases have in store for us.

Non-relational databases are a relatively new technology compared to relational databases. NoSQL or Not-Only SQL allows us to model our data differently to the traditional tabular, relational databases approach.

The key to NoSQL's success is the simplicity of its horizontal scaling and high performance. This high performance comes at a cost. NoSQL sacrifices some of the principles of ACID and does not support Join transactions. This drawback may sound alarming, but it's not an issue for many environments. The pure performance and horizontal scalability that NoSQL databases bring are perfect for commercial (and some enterprise) games.

NoSQL is excellent at managing large volumes of unstructured data, making it ideal for machine learning applications and real-time web applications too!

Horizontal scalability is the actual selling point here for game development. Games evolve; that is especially true for online games as a service. If you need to develop a new update for your game, adding a new item type for a relational database could be a nightmare if the design isn't perfect. With non-relational databases, this is easy to remedy.

Let's take a look at some of the pros and cons of non-relational databases.

Pros of Non-relational Databases

- **Performance** - Non-relational databases are highly performant, especially with read operations.

- **Horizontal scalability** - Possibly one of the most significant benefits to non-relational databases is its horizontal scalability, making it ideal for games where we might need to expand the database to accommodate additional features.

- **Pricing** - Most NoSQL database engines don't have ridiculous pricing structures.

Cons of Non-relational Databases

- **Sacrifices some ACID principles** - This sacrifice makes it unsuitable to some environments, particularly banking. Though, this drawback doesn't affect its uses for game development.

Overall, I'd highly suggest NoSQL databases for most multiplayer games. The scalability and performance are just a win-win in almost every regard. However, there might be some enterprise environments where relational databases make more sense, making it reasonable to keep both in mind.

Let's take a look at some relational and non-relational database engines.

A Few Popular Relational Database Engines

- Oracle

- MySQL

- MSSQL

- PostgreSQL

A Few Popular Non-relational Database Engines

- Amazon DynamoDB

- MongoDB

- Cassandra

For the rest of this chapter, I'll be working with Amazon DynamoDB. It's a powerful NoSQL database engine, which is excellent for scalable, multiplayer games. As a bonus, it's even available on the AWS free tier. So, you can follow along and try it out for yourself.

Using DynamoDB

To follow along with the book, you'll need to head over to the AWS website at https://aws.amazon.com and register yourself an account. AWS has a free tier consisting of three different types of free. AWS Dynamo has the free tier that we're looking for, which is always free.

The Dynamo free tier gives us 25GB of free database storage and enough read/write operations to handle 200 million read/write operations per month.

Let's take a look at Figure 5-3.

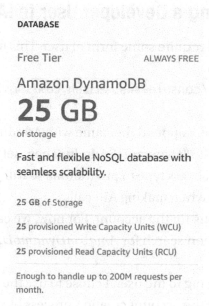

DATABASE

Free Tier   ALWAYS FREE

Amazon DynamoDB

25 GB
of storage

Fast and flexible NoSQL database with
seamless scalability.

25 GB of Storage

25 provisioned Write Capacity Units (WCU)

25 provisioned Read Capacity Units (RCU)

Enough to handle up to 200M requests per
month.

Figure 5-3. *The figure shows Amazon dynamoDB's free-tier features*

Another great benefit to DynamoDB is that Amazon has gone and created a high-level DotNet API!

Installing the AWS DotNet API

The suggested installation method is overly complicated for Unity. That's why I've gone and made a UnityPackage for you to easily import into your project that will handle any assembly definition required by AWS. You can access the package at the following GitHub repo:

`https://github.com/VoidFletcher/UnityAWS-Integration/`

You can clone the repo or download the UnityPackage from the releases section of the repository. Import the unity package, and you're good to go.

Configuring AWS DotNet API

Next, we'll need to perform some configurations.

Creating and Assigning a Developer User to IAM

To access our database, we'll require some form of user. This user should *not* be our main administrative account.

So, head over to `https://console.aws.amazon.com/iamv2/home?#/users`, and click the "Add User" button.

Give the new user a name. I append the name with Admin as this user will fulfill an admin role – something like "DynamoDBAdmin. Then, set the access type to "Programmatic." Setting the access type to programmatic will give us an *access key ID* and a *secret access key* to use when making API calls.

Next, we need permissions for the account. For now, we can simply click "Attach Existing Policies Directly." Then search for *AmazonDynamoDBFullAccess*. Select the permission and proceed.

You can optionally add a tag to the user. I chose to use the Developer tag with no value. Once complete, finish the account creation process by clicking the "Add User" button. You should then see the following screen (Figure 5-4).

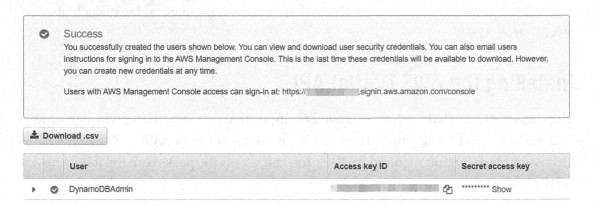

Figure 5-4. *The figure shows your newly created account with its associated access key ID and secret access key*

Configuring the Local Credentials File

For our program to execute any actions, we need to store the credentials of our newly created user. We hold these credentials in a specific directory within a credentials file. You must include this credentials file on any machine with permission to interact with the API.

Let's go ahead and create our credentials file.

Go to *%USERPROFILE%\.aws*, and make the directory if it does not exist. Then create a text file called "credentials." Be sure to remove the text extension, and open it with a text editor of your choice.

Next, we'll want to add the credentials to the file:

```
[default]
aws_access_key_id = <YourAccessKeyHere>
aws_secret_access_key = <YourSecretAccessKeyHere>
```

Insert your access key and secret access key, replacing the preceding placeholders with your appropriate keys. Be sure not to include the triangle brackets. Your key should look something like this:

```
[default]
aws_access_key_id = A***************5
aws_secret_access_key = AM**************1/d***********L
```

The default tag lets the AWS API know to use these credentials if it could not find any other credentials. Finally, go ahead and add the region to the credentials file. You can find these in the Amazon Control Panel at the top right of the toolbar.

I'm in South Africa and plan to host my DynamoDB in Cape Town, South Africa. So, I'll add the following line to my credentials file:

```
region = af-south-1
```

Save the file, and now you have everything in place to get started.

Connecting to the Database from Your Game Server

Next, we'll want to be able to test our connection to the database. We'll do this programmatically. You can find an in-depth example at the following GitHub repo, under the */Examples* directory.

https://github.com/VoidFletcher/UnityAWS-Integration

The AwsDatabaseApi mono behavior can be attached to an object in your scene. I encourage you to open this class and take a deeper look. Let's take a look at the connecting part in more detail:

```
private IAmazonDynamoDB client;
...
```

```
client = new AmazonDynamoDBClient(RegionEndpoint.AFSouth1);
```

All we need to do is create a new *AmazonDynamoDBClient*. Using the standard constructor with our chosen region will attempt to initialize a connection with the default credentials in our credentials file that we created in the previous step.

If you're using the example AwsDatabaseApi behavior from my repo, you should see something like Figure 5-5 in your Unity Editor.

Figure 5-5. *The figure shows the Unity Editor log after successfully connecting to the database*

Now, of course, there won't be any tables in the database since we haven't created any yet.

A question you may have is, "But, I don't remember creating a DynamoDB server?" I know! It just works. DynamoDB doesn't work on the concept of namespaces or instances or databases in the traditional sense. Instead, a DynamoDB is tied to the Account and the region that it's in, which is why a multi-account architecture is a good approach when working with multiple projects or environments. We can also use IAM for fine-grained control on what tables can be accessed.

Now, let's take a look at a few ways that we can populate our database.

Designing the Database

The high-level API that Amazon provides us with gives us access to everything that AWS has to offer. That's why we must have narrowed the permissions granted to our developer user only to have access to DynamoDB. Before we get into using the API to create tables, let's look at the web interface first.

Head over to the DynamoDB control page, found at the following URL:

```
https://console.aws.amazon.com/dynamodb
```

Be sure to set the region to your intended region, specified in the credentials file you created earlier.

You should see a large "Create Table" button. Click that button. DynamoDB will prompt you to give the table a name and a partition key that Dynamo uses to generate the primary key. Dynamo uses a partition key to generate this primary key by hashing it.

I've created a table with the name "Players" and the partition key "PlayerId." Click the "Create" button at the bottom of the window, and jump back into Unity.

Rerun the example, and this time, your Unity Editor Log should look something like Figure 5-6.

Figure 5-6. *The figure shows the Unity Editor log after successfully connecting to the database and discovering our newly created table*

So, what about creating tables via the API? Creating tables via the API is also relatively straightforward.

Firstly, we need a CreateTableRequest object. This object is responsible for holding the data of our request. We then populate the request with the table name, provisioned throughput, its key schema, and the different attributes that the table should hold.

Once done, we can pass the request off to our "IAmazonDynamoDB" object as an async call. Let's take a look at the code from the example in my repo:

```
private async void CreateRandomTable(int tableSuffix)
{
    CreateTableRequest newTable = new CreateTableRequest
    {
        TableName = "NewRandomTable-" + tableSuffix,
        ProvisionedThroughput = new ProvisionedThroughput {
        ReadCapacityUnits = 10,
                                        WriteCapacityUnits = 10 },
        KeySchema = new List<KeySchemaElement>
        {
            new KeySchemaElement
            {
                AttributeName = "KeyId",
                KeyType = KeyType.HASH
```

```
        }
    },
    AttributeDefinitions = new List<AttributeDefinition>
    {
        new AttributeDefinition { AttributeName = "KeyId",
                                  AttributeType = ScalarAttributeType.S
                                },
    }
};

    await client.CreateTableAsync(newTable);
}
```

One thing that isn't clear from IntelliSense is the ScalarAttributeType.

There are three types of ScalarAttributeTypes: S, N, and B. These are String, Number, and Binary, respectively. Let's take a look at their uses:

- **String** - Up to 400KiB of UTF-8 encoded text.

- **Number** - Numeric values made of up to 38 digits (positive, negative, or zero).

- **Binary** - This allows for up to 400KiB of binary data encoded as base64 before sending to DynamoDB.

Running the previous code by right-clicking on the component and selecting "Create Random Table" should yield the following results (Figure 5-7).

Figure 5-7. *The figure shows the Unity Editor log after successfully connecting to the database and creating our new, random table*

Now, if we head back over to the web interface, we can see our newly created table there, too!

Your web interface should have something like Figure 5-8.

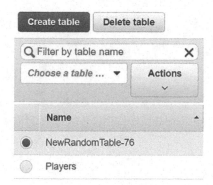

Figure 5-8. *Our new table should now appear in the AWS web interface*

We now have an empty table that we can store data within. If you're familiar with relational databases, you might be curious about why we haven't defined any columns.

In NoSQL, schemaless databases, we don't define the columns themselves, except those used to generate the primary key. These tables are dynamic and can adapt to a wide range of data. That's what makes horizontal scaling so easy. Let's discuss how we can store information in our "Players" table.

Storing Information

Let's start by using the web interface again. Using the web interface provides an excellent way to visualize what we're doing before digging into the API alternative.

Head back over to the web interface, and select the "Players" table. On the right side of the interface, select the "Items" tab, followed by "Create Item" (Figure 5-9). Here, we want to fill out the "PlayerId" field, which makes up our primary key. We can fill in an example email address here as an example. Then, press the "+" icon to the left of it. Select "Insert," and insert a new number into the item.

Figure 5-9. *The Create Item menu in the AWS web interface*

Let's name the number "PlayerDeaths" and give it a value. Press "Save," and you now have a new item within your table.

Now, repeat the same process, adding a new player with a number field. This time, name the number field "PlayerKills" and give it a value. Save the new item, and notice how both of these objects exist within the same table (Figure 5-10).

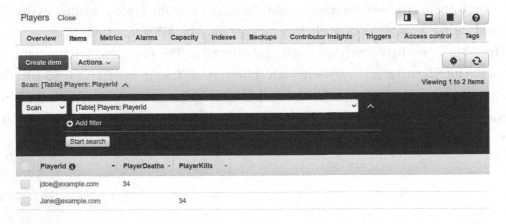

Figure 5-10. *Notice how our table is capable of holding dynamic data in the AWS web interface*

In relational databases, this data would not be possible to hold in a single table without modifying the table's schema first. Horizontal expansion with relational databases gets especially tricky if you're trying to remove columns. Yet, here we are with my favorite NoSQL database. This dynamic data holding makes it ideal for games that will update several times throughout their lifetimes.

Now, let's see how we'd go about doing the same actions but using the AWS API.

Creating new items in a table through the API is where AWS Dynamo shines. It shows off the horizontal scalability of the system.

To get started, we'll need to create a data class for our table item and mark it with the relevant attributes for the API to understand the context of our data. Let's take a look at the following code:

```
[DynamoDBTable("Players")]
public class Player
{
    [DynamoDBHashKey]
    public string PlayerId;

    [DynamoDBProperty("PlayerDeaths")]
    public int PlayerDeaths;

    [DynamoDBProperty("PlayerKills")]
    public int PlayerKills;
}
```

In the class, we're defining the relation between the "Player" class and the "Players" table by adding the "DynamoDBTable" attribute. Then, we decorate the "PlayerId" string with the "DynamoDBHashKey" attribute. The DynamoDBHashKey lets the API know that the "PlayerId" should be used to generate the primary key hash.

That's all you need to get the class set up for the API. However, we still want to save meaningful data in the database. So, we'll need to create some fields for that. Let's stick with the previous example and use "PlayerDeaths" and "PlayerKills" as fields we might want to use for storing data. Finish off by decorating those fields with the "DynamoDBProperty" attribute, and you're all set.

Let's get to adding some data to our database.

Firstly, in our AwsDatabaseApi class, or whatever class you're using to populate your database, we'll need to add a new DynamoDBContext object. This DynamoDBContext object will give our code context on how the Database should look. Let's take a look at the following code:

```
private DynamoDBContext context;
```

Now that we have a DynamoDBContext object, we'll need to populate it with the context of our database by initializing it. You'll want to ensure that you only call this code after you have initialized your IAmazonDynamoDB object:

```
private async void AddNewRandomPlayer()
{
    context = new DynamoDBContext(client);

    Player newPlayer = new Player
    {
        PlayerId = "newPlayer-" + Random.Range(0, 1000),
        PlayerDeaths = Random.Range(0, 30),
        PlayerKills = Random.Range(0, 30)
    };

    await context.SaveAsync<Player>(newPlayer);
}
```

In the code, we're getting the context of our database by using our database client connection. Then we're creating a new player object. That player object is what we decorated with the required attributes.

We can then populate the player object with our required data and call the SaveAsync method of our DynamoDBContext. Once the await call completes, you'll have a newly generated player item in your "Players" table. Again, the significant part about this is that none of the fields, excluding the key, are required. Adding additional fields to our player object will add them to the database as new columns, too!

Retrieving Information

So far, we've learned how to create new items in the database. However, in our examples, we've used the AWSDynamoDB web interface to view our results. Retrieving items from the database via code is essential for our game to function. We'll also need to retrieve our items from the database to update them, which I'll cover later in this chapter.

DynamoDB provides several ways of accessing our data. I'll be covering a few ways of doing so while using the database model workflow, which will ensure that we neatly fit our items into C# data classes. There are ways of retrieving data and table structure from AWS, but those techniques are not as relevant to game development. If you're interested in the low-level API, I'd suggest looking at the documentation found at the following link:

```
https://docs.aws.amazon.com/amazondynamodb/latest/developerguide/
Programming.LowLevelAPI.html
```

We'll be using the high-level interface for our needs. The high-level interface provides us with three main ways of retrieving our data. Which one you use will depend on the situation. Let's take a look at them.

LoadAsync

LoadAsync allows us to grab an item directly from the database using its primary or composite hash key and cast it neatly into a C# data class marked with the relevant DynamoDB Attributes that we covered earlier.

We can use LoadAsync to grab our object as follows:

```
var existingPlayer = await context.LoadAsync<Player>("johndoe");
```

The LoadAsync takes a type, which should be decorated with the appropriate attributes: "DynamoDBTable," "DynamoDBHashKey," and "DynamoDBProperty."

The API then creates a new object of the specified type and matches the data to the fields automatically.

Use LoadAsync when

- You want to get a specific item from your tables.

- You know the primary hash or composite key of the table.

- Want to update an item.

Let's take a look at a few other options for retrieving data using the high-level interface.

QueryAsync

QueryAsync is when you need to get results from a table with a composite key, allowing you to perform a query on the secondary key.

An example of this would be using the player name in conjunction with an identifier to form the unique hash key. Several online services allow a player to have a Name#0001, where the user chooses the Name. The system automatically assigns the number or perhaps changed to an available number chosen by the user. An example of this would be using the player name in conjunction with an identifier to form the unique hash key.

Using Query, you could find all players that match a given name, ignoring the secondary key. Using a composite key with a query would also be more performant than having the display name as a field within the table, as Query is cheaper than Scan, which we'll cover shortly. Query only performs a lookup on the primary and secondary keys.

A Query also allows you to perform various operations on the secondary key, also known as a "sort" or "range" key. Let's take a look at the following code:

```
var players = await context.QueryAsync<CompositePlayer>(name).
GetRemainingAsync();
```

It's important to note that Query will only work on a table that uses a composite key since a table with only a primary key will never have duplicates.

ScanAsync

ScanAsync is a glorified, whole-document search. While being quite performant, if possible, you should prefer Query over Scan, as Scan searches through all data within a table.

A Scan allows you to get a list of results that match the given criteria. Let's take a look at the following code:

```
private Task<List<Player>> GetAllPlayersInDbWithMoreThanXKills(int
kills)
{
    var scanConditions = new[]
    {
        new ScanCondition("PlayerKills", ScanOperator.GreaterThan, kills),
```

```
    };

    return context.ScanAsync<Player>(scanConditions).
    GetRemainingAsync();
}
```

Our query "context.ScanAsync" takes a list or array of "ScanConditions". These scan conditions allow us to filter our scan to get the results that we want.

In the preceding code example, we create a new scan condition that checks each player to see if they match the criteria. In our example, the scan criteria object notifies the scan to look at the "PlayerKills" property and return any results greater than the number of kills specified.

We then get a task containing a list of matching players. We can await the task to use the data. The list should never be null but will be empty if the scan finds no results.

Updating Information

When we're dealing with data that has a lot of change frequency, such as the player kills, it's essential to know how to update the information for our already-existing players in the database.

To update an object in the database, we'll need to grab a copy of it from the database, ensure that it exists, update any fields that we'd like to change on the object, and finally pass it back into the database.

Let's test this with some code and see the update. If you're using my example, then right-click on the AWSDatabaseApi component, and choose "CreateDemoUser":

```
private async void CreateDemoPlayerInDb()
{
    var newPlayer = new Player
    {
        PlayerId = "Demo Player",
        PlayerDeaths = 3,
        PlayerKills = 0
    };

    await context.SaveAsync(newPlayer);
}
```

The code will generate a new user with the player ID of "Demo Player." We then assign three deaths, and zero kills to the player. Let's run that code, and check in on our DynamoDB web interface. Let's take a look at Figure 5-11 to see our results.

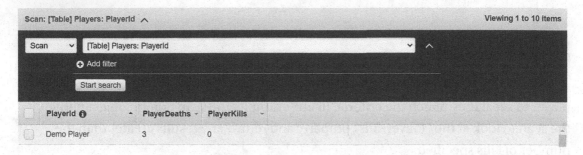

Figure 5-11. *The figure shows our demo player item in the "players" table*

There is our player, with three deaths and no kills. Let's update the player's kills. If you're using my example, right-click the AWSDatabaseApi component, and choose "Update Demo Player Kills Randomly."

Let's take a look at the following code to see what's happening:

```
private async void UpdateDemoPlayerKillsRandomly()
{
    var existingPlayer = await context.LoadAsync<Player>("Demo Player");

    if (existingPlayer == null)
    {
        Debug.LogError("Demo player does not exist yet.");
        return;
    }

    existingPlayer.PlayerKills = Random.Range(1, 1000);

    await context.SaveAsync(existingPlayer);
}
```

Here, we find the existing player object by hash key using "context.LoadAsync" with the type "Player." We then update the "player kills" value, and pass the object back into our database using "context.SaveAsync".

Let's head back to our DynamoDB web interface to see our changes.

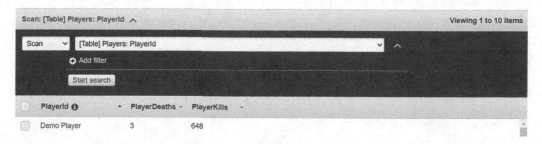

Figure 5-12. *The figure shows our demo player item in the "players" table with an updated "playerKills" value*

In Figure 5-12, we can see the player now has the original three deaths but this time has a different number of kills. Updating items is as simple as that. You can execute the "Update Demo Player Kills Randomly" context menu option to see the item updated in the AWS DynamoDB dashboard.

Serving Content to Your Players

During the lifecycle of a game, you'll be dealing with the database on several occasions. With that said, database calls are not free – both in performance and eventually, with cost. As such, you should always try to minimize your database calls and use Query instead of Scan where possible.

Most importantly, you should only ever make database calls from a dedicated server that you control. Any calls from the client will fail due to the client not having the appropriate credentials and will incur a performance hit.

Suppose you're developing a host-based game with persistence handled by your company. In that case, you should consider having an intermediary server that can provide a point of authority and access the permitted data.

Some Closing Notes for AWS API

The Amazon Suite is extremely extensive, and I've skipped many of the tools and features that it provides. The AWS API allows access to every one of these tools and services.

If you'd like to find out more about these API calls, be sure to have a look at the following documentation:

```
https://docs.aws.amazon.com/dynamodb/?id=docs_gateway
```

CHAPTER 6

Scaling Up, A Lot

By now, you should be pretty comfortable with building multiplayer games in Unity, but that's only half the battle. Next, we'll discuss how you can scale your multiplayer game or product to reach an expanding audience. Scaling is something many companies have struggled with in the past, and sometimes, you just cannot anticipate the success of your game. I'm looking at you, "Among Us" and "Splitgate."

The fact is, servers cost money, and many servers cost a lot of money. Before launching, it would be wise to ensure that your company has enough liquidity to accommodate viral growth. That's not to say that your game will be the next viral sensation, but it's vital to plan for different outcomes. A game launch that is too successful can almost be as devastating as a fizzled launch if your eager players get bored of waiting for you to put infrastructure in place.

At the same time, throwing all of your money at new servers can cause your company to hemorrhage money – this is especially bad if your user retention or customer value is low.

Typically, when hosting, you can acquire two kinds of servers: shared hosting and dedicated hosting, often referred to as bare-metal hosting. Each of these has its pros and cons. In this chapter, I'll discuss hosting and scaling your game servers to meet viral demand.

Let's start by taking a look at two prime examples of viral games that exploded:

- Among Us
- Splitgate

These two games are prime examples of viral growth.

D. Engelbrecht, *Building Multiplayer Games in Unity*, https://doi.org/10.1007/978-1-4842-7474-3_6

Viral Game Studies

How Among Us Became a Part of Us

Among Us – Developed and Published by InnerSloth

Among Us was a viral sensation, turning friends on each other in a unique social deduction game. The game pits between 4 and 15 players with each other. The goal of the game differs on your role, automatically assigned during the start of a game.

Upon starting, the game assigns you to a team, either a crewmate just trying to live his life or a hellish creature disguised as a crewmate, known as the imposter. As a crewmate, your goal is to complete tasks before the imposter devours your fellow crewmates. There's a catch, though. Only you know what you are – and it's up to you and the other players to determine which players seem sus (suspicious).

As an imposter, your goal is to kill off any crewmates without seeming suspicious.

During gameplay points, there is voting, where players vote on which player to cast out. If players vote out all imposters, then the crewmates win. If there is only a single crewmate remaining, then the imposters win.

That sums up the game, which is quite simple at its core. So, how many players did Among Us have? Well, chances are, you already know what I've just told you or, at the very least, know the name.

Among Us had a peak of over 500,000,000 monthly active users. At the end of August 2020, they peaked over 438,000 weekly active users on Steam alone.

So, how long did it take to reach such an insane userbase? Well, that's the thing; nearly two months prior, Among Us had less than 7000 weekly active users. That's 431,000 weekly active user growth in 2 months.

That's nearly 30,000 game rooms running in a world where the players filled all rooms with 15 players. So, the number of game instances is likely way higher. That's just with Steam alone, not to mention the Android launch that took the game to a peak of over 500,000,000 monthly active users.

Let's take a look at the Steam graphs for Among Us (Figure 6-1).

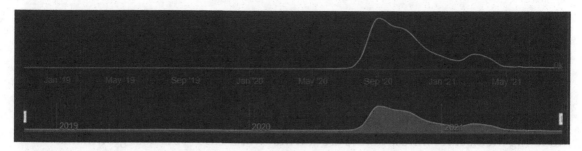

Figure 6-1. *The figure shows the dramatic spike in users over time when Among Us went viral*

It's important to note that your user count won't always be a smooth growth curve. In fact, in many viral cases, you'll only have days or weeks to react to exponential demand before seeing a decline in concurrent users. That's why it's important to always prepare for the possibility of exponential growth curves.

Buying out a year of hosting space targeted at your peak is a bad idea too. We want our servers to dynamically adjust, saving costs after the peak in our game's lifecycle or scaling back up as needed in the case of Path of Exile, which experiences significant spikes in player counts at the release of each expansion. Let's take a look at how Grinding Gear Games' Path of Exile player count spikes (Figure 6-2) looks like for comparison.

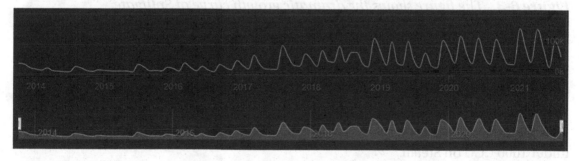

Figure 6-2. *The figure shows how Path of Exile (GGG) experiences regular spikes in its player count at the release of each new expansion*

We'll discuss how we can handle situations where player count fluctuates later in this chapter. For now, let's move on to another viral game study – Splitgate.

"Halo Meets Portal"

Splitgate – Developed and Published by 1047 Games

Splitgate is a fast-paced arena PVP shooter game developed by 1047 Games, and it's an exciting game to model a viral game study around.

The reason for that is because 1047 Games used a similar approach to this book, modeling their server infrastructure around the "worst-case" viral user growth that Among Us experienced. It's essential to follow their journey, as sometimes, you just can't anticipate the growth of your game.

Splitgate's growth dramatically exceeded that of Among Us in terms of timescale (Figure 6-3). Let's take a look at their user graphs to see what I mean.

Figure 6-3. *The figure shows the dramatic growth curve of Splitgate*

The user growth of Splitgate is vastly sharper than that of Among Us, but you might ask: Why is the concurrent user count plateauing around 60K CCU? That's a great question, and the answer may surprise you.

The growth of Splitgate has been so unexpected that the developers have had to limit their player count to relieve server strain, simply because 2 months prior, the game had under 1000 CCU on Steam.

That's roughly 7000% user growth in 2 months.

Let's take a look at the numbers in greater detail (Figure 6-4).

Month	Avg. Players	Gain	% Gain	Peak Players
Last 30 Days	*23,976.5*	*+20,261.5*	*+545.40%*	*67,724*
July 2021	3,715.0	+3,378.6	+1004.20%	45,597
June 2021	336.4	+119.3	+54.98%	954
May 2021	217.1	-34.1	-13.57%	401
April 2021	251.2	+4.0	+1.64%	433
March 2021	247.1	+44.4	+21.92%	444
February 2021	202.7	-32.8	-13.92%	377

Figure 6-4. *The figure explores the player count of Splitgate in greater detail*

Splitgate is quite a new game to the public eye, so it will be interesting to follow further.

With that said, it does make an excellent point – modeling your game around the most dramatic user growth curve that you can find won't guarantee that your game won't be overwhelmed. And in many cases, your product won't experience such dramatic user growth curves. There are many factors to take into consideration when modeling your "worst-case" expected growth curves.

If you're launching a custom enterprise product targeting a specific client, for example, you're likely only going to have to deal with a maximum userbase of that client's company.

If you're launching a commercial game that has a very niche audience, chances are you'll have time to scale your servers. Either way, it's always essential to understand what can happen when releasing an ideal game in a perfect market with a high chance for viral user growth.

So how do we go about hosting our game servers and, more importantly, deciding what hosting style to use depending on our product?

Let's dive deeper into hosting.

Hosting Servers

There are many different styles of game server hosting available to us, though these generally fall into two categories, shared and dedicated hosting. Each of them has its pros and cons that are important to factor into our decision. Let's take a look at these in greater detail.

Shared/Virtual Hosting

Shared hosting is the practice of sharing hosting space on a given server. It's typically cheaper than the other hosting options for small-scale servers, such as development environments or websites.

Typically, we use a service sold as a VPS (Virtual Private Server) for small-scale game servers such as the recent example. In environments like these, we have access to a virtual machine, which is an isolated environment located on the same physical hardware that other customers of the provider might use. This shared hardware allows the hosting provider to share the burden of cost between all of their clients, reducing the fees you pay.

This shared cost is excellent. However, if other customers have a great demand, it could negatively impact the performance of your environment. In development environments, these impacts are negligible – and if you go with one of the larger hosting providers (AWS, Google, Azure), they have mostly mitigated these effects at a higher cost.

Let's take a look at how shared hosting looks at a conceptual level in Figure 6-5.

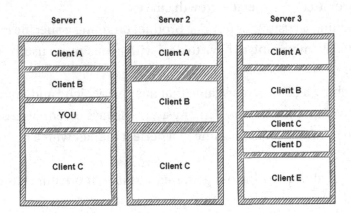

Figure 6-5. *The figure shows shared hosting at a conceptual level*

The real issue here is scalability. If you need to scale to thousands of game servers, this model falls flat on its face, though there is an exception to this that I'll discuss shortly.

Let's compare the pros and cons of this model.

Pros

- Cheap and easy to get started.

- Suitable for small independent studios.

- Suitable for development environments.

- Ideal for webserver hosting.

- Suitable for small player-run game servers.

- Easy to get started.

Cons

- Terrible for scalability with small hosting providers.

- Can suffer performance hits if the shared resource is congested.

Amazon Web Services EC2 is one of the major exceptions to the rule – with significant infrastructure improvements in place to reduce the cons – though at a higher cost than many smaller hosting providers. The same applies to Google Cloud Hosting and Microsoft Azure.

So, what are the alternatives? Let's dig into dedicated hosting next.

Dedicated Hosting/Bare-Metal

Dedicated hosting takes shared hosting to the next level by alleviating the unknown demand of other customers on the given hardware by directly allocating hardware to a client. In dedicated hosting, each customer has direct access to their dedicated servers' hardware, typically allowing for the fine-tuning of GPU and CPU resources.

Bare-metal servers get their name from this direct access to hardware, where the provider does not wrap the server instance within a virtualization technology.

Let's take a look at how dedicated hosting looks at a conceptual level in Figure 6-6:

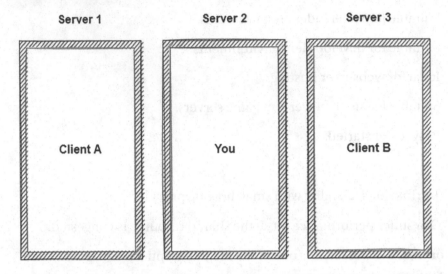

Figure 6-6. *The figure shows dedicated hosting at a conceptual level*

Dedicated hosts are typically faster than shared environments but do come at a higher cost with many smaller hosting providers. Let's take a look at some of the pros and cons.

Pros

- Significantly higher performance compared to shared hosting

- More control over hardware fine-tuning

Cons

- Longer provisioning times

- Higher cost compared to shared hosting with smaller hosting providers

The longer provisioning times and high cost associated with dedicated hosting using smaller providers can make it unsuitable for games with fluctuating player counts or games where you provision your servers on a per-match basis.

So, What Is the Best Option for Hosting Then?

Sadly, there is no one-size-fits-all answer for this question. It honestly depends on the needs of your product, how much scalability you're expecting to need, and what kind of a budget you have.

If you have the budget and need to scale, I recommend shared servers provisioned from AWS, Google Cloud, or Microsoft Azure – but which one, you ask? All of them. Later, in this chapter, I'll discuss the Unity Multiplay service that will help you leverage these three providers for the best possible bang for your buck.

Suppose you have a smaller budget without as much need for scalability in the immediate future. In that case, local hosting providers are a good choice – or even consider using your hosting setup with old server hardware if you're looking to stretch the money. All you need is a few old PC boxes, a great Internet connection with a static public IP address, and some network configuration experience.

Interestingly enough, the critically acclaimed studio Digital Extremes used in-house dedicated machines to host Warframe in its early days.

Since I'm focusing on scalability for this book, we'll focus more on cloud hosting, but before we discuss Unity Multiplay, let's look at each of the individual major hosting providers.

Using Cloud Services to Host Your Game Servers

Cloud hosting is an excellent choice for hosting scalable multiplayer games with global reach, typically allowing you to scale your game to many different regions, reducing network latency and inversely improving the player experience.

It's also ideal for games that have erratic concurrent user counts. Large cloud hosts typically allow you to provision new servers as you need them and possibly, more importantly, decommission servers as you stop needing them – saving your company money in the process.

I'll be covering the Holy Trinity of cloud hosting providers. Amazon, Google, and Microsoft. These are big names that you'll already know, but perhaps you thought of Amazon as a large online shop, or Google as a search engine, or Microsoft as your operating system provider. These three companies house an incredible array of online hosting services, from the DynamoDB that we discussed in a previous chapter to dedicated machine learning platforms.

Let's start with AWS or Amazon Web Services.

AWS – Amazon Web Services

Amazon Web Services is Amazon's suite of hosting tools. In a previous chapter, we covered Amazon DynamoDB, providing our multiplayer game with an easy, scalable, and fast database solution. Now we'll cover EC2, also known as Elastic Cloud Compute.

AWS EC2 is an instance-based hosting solution. Each virtual machine allocated to you is known as an instance. Each instance is hosting within a virtual cloud network, providing direct access to the AWS backbone, allowing for insanely fast inter-server communication between AWS products. EC2 suits a wide variety of needs, from number-crunching to what matters to us – game server hosting.

EC2 also allows us to deploy to regions, configure advanced security policies, and much more.

As a bonus, AWS provides year-long access to free-tier EC2 instances. This free-tier access means you can try it out without paying a cent – though it's worth mentioning that the free-tier server does have limited CPU availability. At the time of writing, it provides two vCPUs and 1GB of RAM.

There are four pricing options available for EC2, each with its benefits depending on your situation. Let's explore each of these in greater detail.

On-Demand

On-demand pricing is what you'd use for games when using EC2. The on-demand pricing structure allows you to rent a server at any given point in time at a given cost per hour.

You can take a look at the pricing using the following URL address:

```
https://aws.amazon.com/ec2/pricing/on-demand/
```

Spot Instances

Spot instances are not always ideal for games when manually provisioning due to the uncertainty of availability. With that said, what are spot instances? They're essentially Amazon's way of saying, "Hey, we have too many servers available!" allowing you to access server space at dramatically reduced prices.

Amazon advertises that this price can be up to 90% less than on-demand pricing, although I've never personally experienced as much of a price drop.

Amazon lets users bid for available server space with spot pricing, allowing you to auto-provision servers if the price drops below a certain threshold. Clients who need cheap number-crunching typically use spot-pricing, especially when server availability is not a significant concern.

You can create a custom image of your server and then have it loaded onto spot servers, where your custom image can have a program launch on boot. Generally, you won't directly use spot instances for game server hosting. If you do, I'd only suggest using it to supplement existing resources since game server availability is critical when providing multiplayer games as a service to your customers.

Savings Plans

Savings plans are excellent if you have a large initial budget, allowing you to provision servers for a set time frame at some discount. Again, it's worth mentioning – provisioning for your peak player count expectancy is a bad idea and could result in hemorrhaging money for your company.

Instead, it would be wise to monitor player counts over a given period and find a stable player count that you'd like to support using EC2 servers on a savings plan, reducing costs for servers that you would anyway be hosting.

You can view these saving plans with the following URL:

```
https://aws.amazon.com/savingsplans/compute-pricing/
```

Let's talk about dedicated hosting with Amazon.

Dedicated Hosting

Dedicated hosting is much like what we discussed at the start of this chapter, though with Amazon, it works a bit differently. Instead of charging more, Amazon charges less for bare-metal server rental. Think of dedicated hosting with Amazon as the extreme version of the savings plan.

Using AWS dedicated hosting for game development can be an excellent approach for serving the stable userbase. Still, due to the nature of games and the fluctuating player counts, I'd suggest a hybrid approach to dedicated and on-demand hosting.

You can take a look at the dedicated hosting costs here:

```
https://aws.amazon.com/ec2/dedicated-hosts/pricing/.
```

Getting Started with EC2

Let's take a look at how you can get started with AWS EC2.

Registering/Logging In

To get started, you'll need an AWS account. If you followed the DynamoDB part of the book, then you'll already have an AWS account. If not, you can create an AWS account (Figure 6-7) using the following URL:

```
https://portal.aws.amazon.com/billing/signup
```

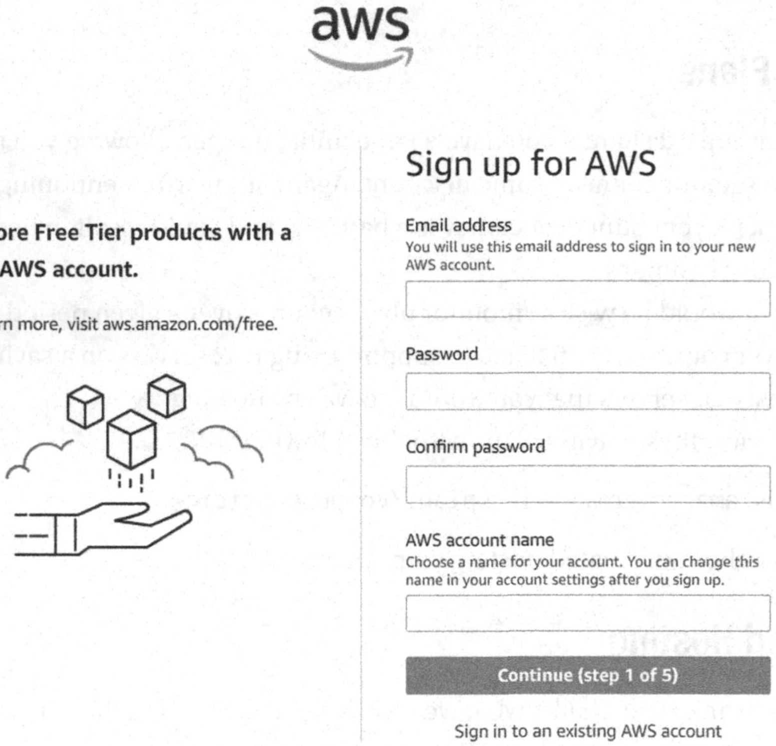

Sign up for AWS

Explore Free Tier products with a new AWS account.

To learn more, visit aws.amazon.com/free.

Email address
You will use this email address to sign in to your new AWS account.

Password

Confirm password

AWS account name
Choose a name for your account. You can change this name in your account settings after you sign up.

Continue (step 1 of 5)

Sign in to an existing AWS account

Figure 6-7. *The AWS account signup screen*

Once you have an account, sign in to your AWS console, and head over to
Services ➤ Compute ➤ EC2

From here, we have access to the Elastic Cloud Compute control panel, allowing us to monitor, launch, terminate, and perform many additional actions to our EC2 instances.

Let's go ahead and launch an instance.

Launching an Instance

Launching an instance itself is incredibly easy (Figure 6-8). Simply select the Instances tab, and then choose "Launch Instances" on the right.

Figure 6-8. *The figure shows the AWS EC2 instances panel*

Selecting launch instances will bring up the instance launch wizard, which will guide you through launching an EC2 instance. This process consists of the following steps:

- **Choose AMI** - An AMI is essentially a snapshot or a template of software configuration. It represents an image that we can load onto a given virtual machine. You can create your own AMI with game server configuration, but you'll first need a Windows AMI. Go ahead, and choose the latest Windows Server base release.

- **Choose instance type** - Here, you'll choose the hardware configuration of your server. If you're using AWS free-tier to try this out, ensure that you use a free-tier eligible hardware configuration. At the time of writing, this would be a T2.micro instance.

- **Configure instance** - Next, you'll have many options available relating to the configuration of your instance. For now, just leaving these defaults is perfectly fine, and these can be changed at a later point if needed. A useful option here is "Enable termination protection," making it harder to terminate your instance accidentally.

- **Add storage** - This allows for the provisioning of additional storage capacity. We can also do this during runtime with zero downtime. If you provision extra storage while your server is running, you will need to access disc management and assign the space to a new or existing partition.

- **Add tags** - Next up, we can assign tags. Tags are case-sensitive key-value pairs that we can use to identify AWS resources for easier management. Tags are entirely optional, and you can skip them for now. In the future, you can look at tagging your servers by Release and Development.

- **Configure security groups** - One of the most important options available to us is the security group configuration. Security groups are essentially your AWS firewall before your Windows Firewall. Ensure that you configure the correct incoming ports and allow the server to communicate outward on the required ports. If you do not complete this step correctly, you will not be able to connect to your game server, you will not be able to remote desktop into your machine, and you won't be able to browse the Web on your virtual machine.

  Security Groups is one of the first configurations that I revisit if I have any unexpected behavior. A good rule of thumb is

  - Ensure that port 3389 incoming is allowed from all IP addresses, later restricted to whitelisted IP addresses. This rule will enable us to use a remote desktop connection to connect to our virtual machine.

  - Enable all outgoing traffic, which is helpful for an initial configuration where you might need to browse the Web from the virtual machine.

  - Enable your incoming game server port from all IP addresses. Setting this rule will allow game clients to connect to your game server.

- **Review** - Finally, we can review our configurations for any changes that we may have missed.

Connecting to Your Instance

To connect to your new instance, we'll be using a remote desktop connection with Windows Remote Desktop.

To connect to your instance, you'll want to head over to the instances panel of your EC2 dashboard. From here, you can select your newly launched instance. The instance may take a few minutes to complete the initial setup, but once it says "Ready," you'll be able to connect.

Right-click your instance and select connect. Doing so will bring up the connect dialogue, as seen in Figure 6-9.

Connect to instance Info

Connect to your instance i-(████████████████████████) using any of these options

| Session Manager | RDP client | EC2 Serial Console |

You can connect to your Windows instance using a remote desktop client of your choice, and by downloading and running the RDP shortcut file below:

> **Download remote desktop file**

When prompted, connect to your instance using the following details:

Public DNS   User name

⬚ ec2-████████ ████████ ████████.com   ⬚ Administrator

Password   **Get password**

If you've joined your instance to a directory, you can use your directory credentials to connect to your instance.

Figure 6-9. *The figure shows the AWS EC2 connect panel*

The panel will provide you with a download link for the remote desktop connection. This downloaded file acts as an RDP shortcut. You'll still need your password, which we'll retrieve next.

Press the "Get Password" link. The first time you do this, AWS will prompt you to download and save a ".PEM" file. This file is essential, and you'll want to save this to a safe location and consider making a backup.

Next, you can use the PEM file to decrypt the Windows password. Copy the Windows password and run your RDP shortcut.Ignore any certificate warnings. These are because AWS uses self-signed certificates by default. Continue and connect to your instance. Next, you will see a familiar Windows desktop window. This window is your remote machine to where you can install your game server. Let's discuss Windows configuration next.

Windows Configuration

Now that we have an EC2 virtual machine, we'll need to do the Windows-side configuration. This step includes everything from installing our game server and any auto-run scripts that we may need – to open the appropriate firewall ports.

You'll want to ensure that you do the following steps:

- **Install your game server** - You can copy/paste to transfer files from your development machine over to your remote server. Alternatively, if you have the server files hosted in a secure location, you can go ahead and download them.

- **Open the appropriate Windows Firewall ports** - Much like we did with the security groups, you'll want to allow incoming connections on the ports that your game server uses.

- **Consider creating adding your game server to Windows startup** - While not strictly needed for development, generally, you'll need to add your game server to the list of applications that launch during Windows startup. You can do this easily by pressing Windows Key + R, then typing "shell:startup" into the Run dialog. Then copy a shortcut to your game server to the newly opened folder.

Finally, you'll want to try to connect to your game server from your local game client. If everything connects, then you're good to go! If you cannot join, recheck your security groups and Windows Firewall configuration. Also, ensure that you can connect to your local game server with a local game client to ensure that your game server is not the problem.

Creating an AMI

By creating an AMI, you can take a snapshot of your Windows environment. The created AMI includes your game server and firewall port rules, making it incredibly easy to launch new EC2 instances with your game server running.

To create an AMI, right-click your instance, go to Image, then "Create Image."

Amazon recommends allowing AWS to shut down the instance for the duration of the AMI creation process to avoid any data corruption on your new AMI.

Once done, the server will start back up – and if you head over to the EC2 AMI control panel, you'll see your newly created image, which you can choose when launching new instances.

Terminating Your Instance

Knowing how to terminate an instance is almost as important as knowing how to create one. If you're no longer using an instance, you can terminate it – different from shutting down an instance. An instance that is in the "Stopped" state will still incur some minor charges for storage. If you'd like to get rid of an instance, you can terminate it.

Simply select your instance, go to "Actions," and click terminate.

Google Cloud

Google Cloud or the Google Cloud Platform (GCP) is the Google equivalent of AWS.

Much like AWS, Google also provides a free trial in the form of $300 worth of free credits. This free trial is ideal for trying out the GCP to see if it's better suited for your needs. It's worth noting that the Google free trial does not include licensing fees for Windows server instances.

You can try out the GCP using the following link: `https://cloud.google.com/pricing/`.

The setup process is quite similar to AWS, and many of the concepts are shared. You'll want to head over to the Google Cloud Console's compute engine panel. From here, you can create a new instance.

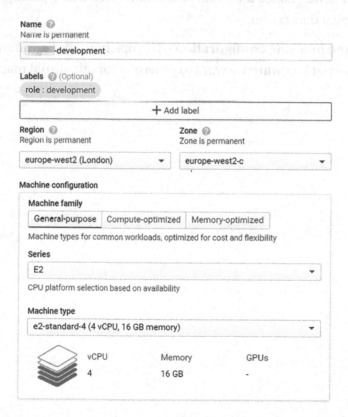

Figure 6-10. *The figure shows the first section of the GCP new instance wizard*

The new instance wizard (Figures 6-10 and 6-11) will require us to complete the following:

- **Give the instance a name** - This is a human-friendly name that we can use to identify the instance. Naming our instance is helpful if we have multiple instances running.

- **Optionally add a key/value pair tag** - Much like AWS, this provides us with an optional label that can help identify the purpose of the instance. We can use this for specific group actions.

- **Select a region** - This will determine what area our endpoint is situated at, typically a geographic location.

- **Select a zone** - Zones are subdivisions of regions that typically represent a data center.

- **Select the machine configuration** - The machine configuration defines what hardware we want to provision for our virtual machine.

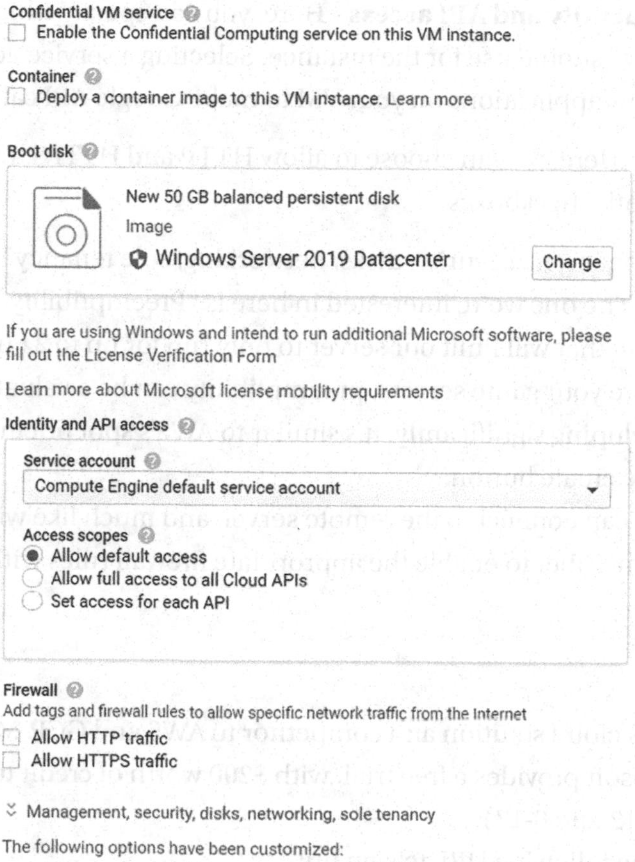

Confidential VM service ⓘ
☐ Enable the Confidential Computing service on this VM instance.

Container ⓘ
☐ Deploy a container image to this VM instance. Learn more

Boot disk ⓘ

New 50 GB balanced persistent disk

Image

🛡 Windows Server 2019 Datacenter   [Change]

If you are using Windows and intend to run additional Microsoft software, please fill out the License Verification Form

Learn more about Microsoft license mobility requirements

Identity and API access ⓘ

Service account ⓘ

Compute Engine default service account   ▾

Access scopes ⓘ
● Allow default access
○ Allow full access to all Cloud APIs
○ Set access for each API

Firewall ⓘ
Add tags and firewall rules to allow specific network traffic from the Internet
☐ Allow HTTP traffic
☐ Allow HTTPS traffic

⌄ Management, security, disks, networking, sole tenancy

The following options have been customized:

Figure 6-11. *The figure shows the last section of the GCP new instance wizard*

- **Optionally enable "Confidential VM Service"** - This is an optional service in which the memory of the VM becomes encrypted to add another layer of security, where even Google would be unable to access the memory. Memory encryption is typically only used for extremely sensitive applications, and we can leave this disabled to save on cost and performance.

- **Optionally deploy a container to the VM** - This is useful if you have a docker container image ready.

- **Specify your boot disc and OS** - Here, we can specify the size of our boot disk and choose an operating system to use. Google includes licensing fees for the operating system selected.

- **Specify identity and API access** - Here, you can specify which account we should use for the instance. Selecting a service account allows your applications on your VM to make Google API calls.

- **Firewall** - Here, we can choose to allow HTTP and HTTPS traffic. Enable both checkboxes.

Selecting "Management, security, disks, networking, sole tenancy" will show additional options. The one we're interested in here is "Preemptibility." Preemptibility is an optional selection that will limit our server to only run for up to 24 hours. Depending on how you structure your game servers, preemptibility can be a valuable option to save on costs while developing significantly. It's similar to AWS's spot pricing.

Finally, click the create button.

From here, you can connect to the remote server, and much like with the AWS server, it's important to remember to enable the appropriate firewall rules within Windows!

Azure

Azure is Microsoft's cloud solution and competitor to AWS and GCP. Much like its competitors, Microsoft provides a free trial, with $200 worth of credit to use in your first 30 days (Figures 6-12 and 6-13).

Head over to the following URL to sign up:

`https://azure.microsoft.com/account/free`

Once you've completed the account creation and verification process, you'll have access to the Azure portal.

Select the burger menu at the top left, and choose "Virtual Machines" from the drop-down list. Then select "Create Instance." You should see the following diagram:

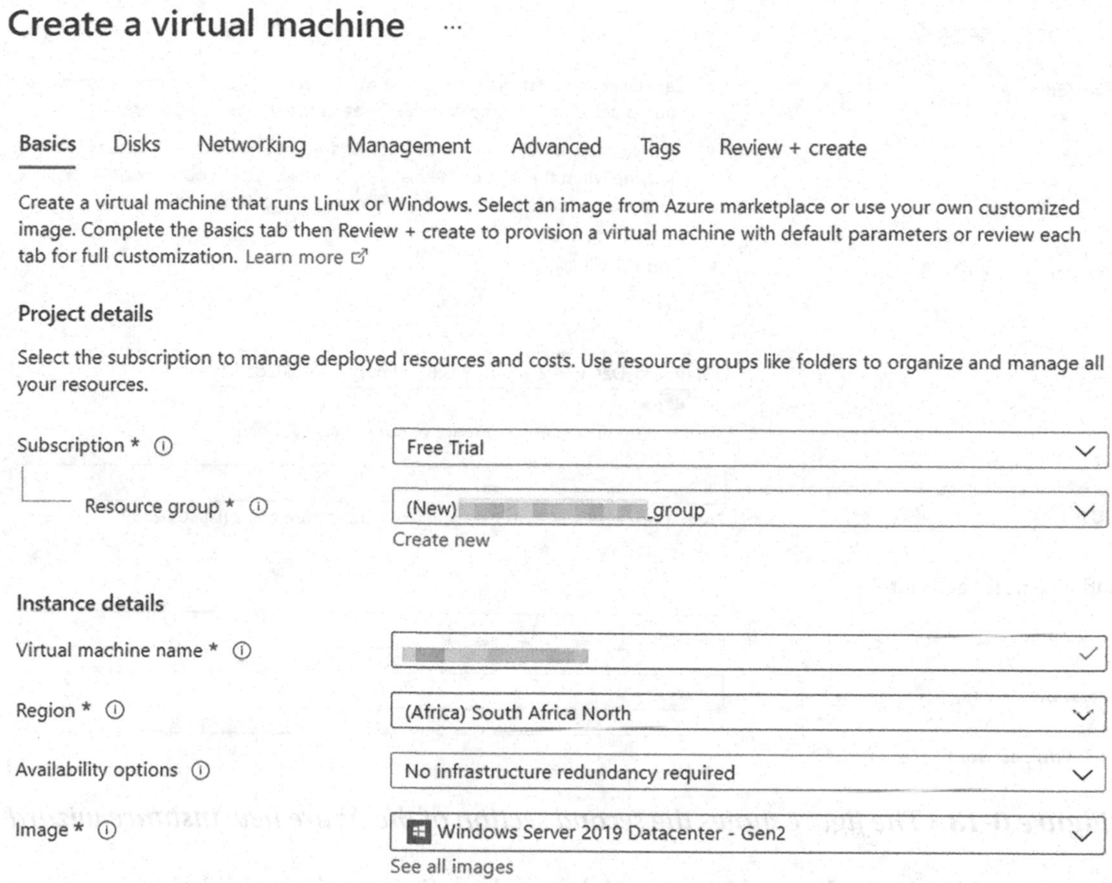

Create a virtual machine   ...

Basics   Disks   Networking   Management   Advanced   Tags   Review + create

Create a virtual machine that runs Linux or Windows. Select an image from Azure marketplace or use your own customized image. Complete the Basics tab then Review + create to provision a virtual machine with default parameters or review each tab for full customization. Learn more ⬀

Project details

Select the subscription to manage deployed resources and costs. Use resource groups like folders to organize and manage all your resources.

Subscription * ⓘ

| Free Trial | ⌄ |

Resource group * ⓘ

| (New) ▓▓▓▓▓▓▓▓▓▓▓▓▓_group | ⌄ |
Create new

Instance details

Virtual machine name * ⓘ

| ▓▓▓▓▓▓▓ | ✓ |

Region * ⓘ

| (Africa) South Africa North | ⌄ |

Availability options ⓘ

| No infrastructure redundancy required | ⌄ |

Image * ⓘ

| ⊞ Windows Server 2019 Datacenter - Gen2 | ⌄ |
See all images

Figure 6-12. *The figure shows the first section of the Azure new instance wizard*

Here, you'll want to complete the following:

- **Select your subscription** - This determines how Azure will bill you. We can use the Free Trial subscription to test this process out.

- **Name your server instance** - Give your server instance a name that you can recognize.

- **Set your server region** - Set the region where you'd like Azure to provision your server.

- **Select a server image** - Select a server image, or a snapshot of the OS, much like AWS AMIs.

191

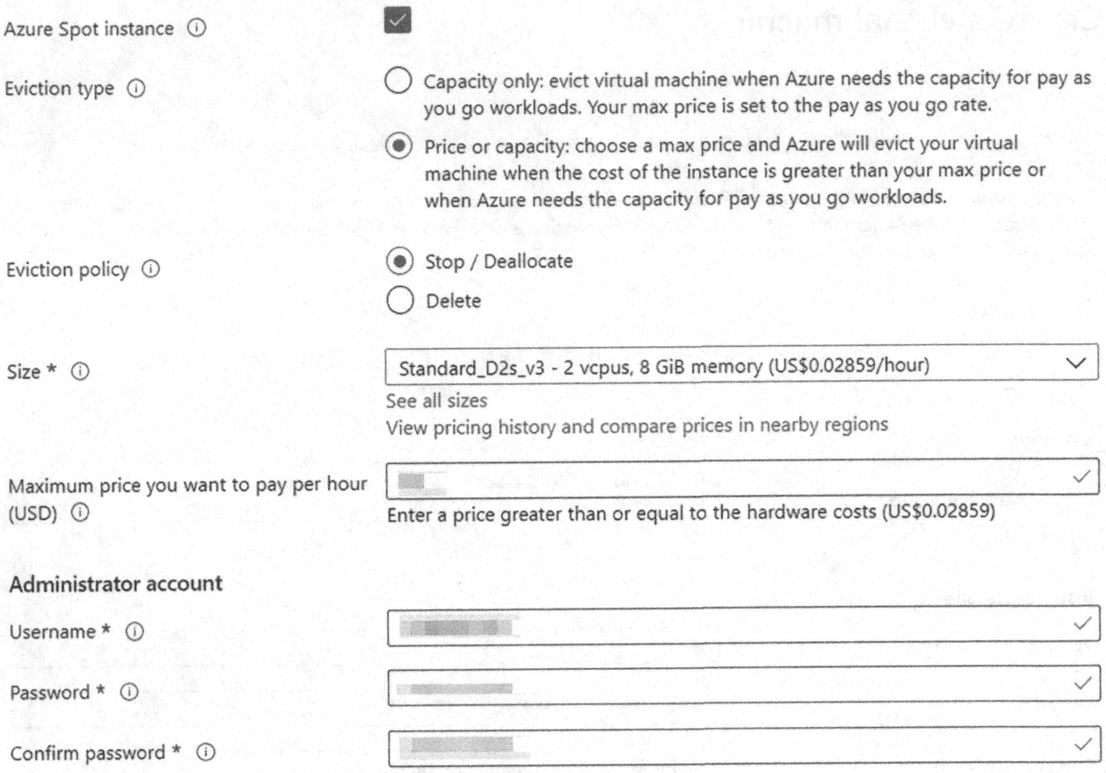

Azure Spot instance ⓘ   ☑

Eviction type ⓘ   ◯ Capacity only: evict virtual machine when Azure needs the capacity for pay as
                                             you go workloads. Your max price is set to the pay as you go rate.

                                          ⦿ Price or capacity: choose a max price and Azure will evict your virtual
                                             machine when the cost of the instance is greater than your max price or
                                             when Azure needs the capacity for pay as you go workloads.

Eviction policy ⓘ   ⦿ Stop / Deallocate
                                          ◯ Delete

Size * ⓘ | Standard_D2s_v3 - 2 vcpus, 8 GiB memory (US$0.02859/hour)   ⌄ |
                                          See all sizes
                                          View pricing history and compare prices in nearby regions

Maximum price you want to pay per hour | ▮▮▮▮   ✓ |
(USD) ⓘ   Enter a price greater than or equal to the hardware costs (US$0.02859)

Administrator account

Username * ⓘ | ▮▮▮▮▮   ✓ |

Password * ⓘ | ▮▮▮▮▮▮   ✓ |

Confirm password * ⓘ | ▮▮▮▮▮   ✓ |

Figure 6-13. *The figure shows the second section of the Azure new instance wizard*

- **Alternatively, enable spot pricing and configure eviction policies and bid prices** - This will allow you to take advantage of spot pricing, ideal for environments where you don't care if the server goes down.

- **Configure administrator account credentials** - Choose your administrator account username and password.

Next, be sure to look at the "Networking" tab at the top. The networking tab will offer additional settings; be sure to select "Advanced" on the "NIC network security group."

We're explicitly looking to creating a new security group. Let's begin with an inbound rule for our game server (Figure 6-14). We'll want to allow the port that our game server communicates on.

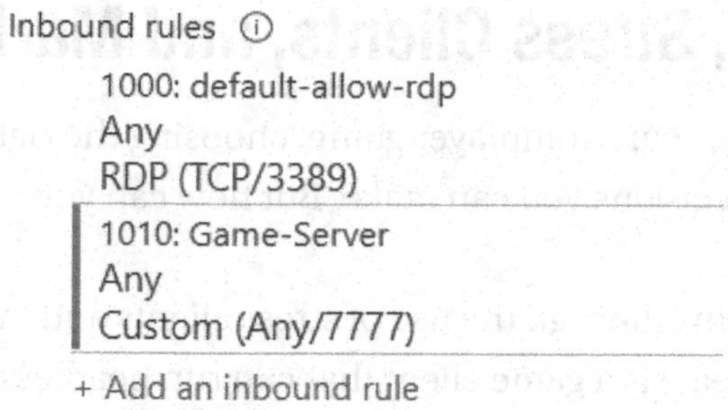

Inbound rules ⓘ

1000: default-allow-rdp
Any
RDP (TCP/3389)

1010: Game-Server
Any
Custom (Any/7777)

+ Add an inbound rule

Figure 6-14. *The figure shows our newly created inbound port rule*

Finally, click the "Review + Create" button. Azure servers take quite a while to provision, but you'll have a new server to use once the process is complete.

Unity Multiplay

Unity Multiplay is by far one of the best hosting solutions out there for large, scalable multiplayer games. Unity Multiplay is essentially a pricing engine that grabs the best available price from the hosts that we just discussed and launches your game servers at the best rates.

It's scalable and can handle millions of players. Major studios, including Respawn Entertainment with their incredibly successful "Apex Legends," use Unity Multiplay, where Multiplay helped Respawn scale 50 million players in 24 days.

Unity Multiplay is not as easily accessible as directly hosting with the previous hosting providers, though. Still, if you're expecting a massive launch or need for scalability, you can contact the Multiplay team over at the following URL:

`https://create.unity3d.com/multiplay-contact-us`

The Multiplay team is accommodating and will guide you through the process and provide additional valuable insight throughout your game launch.

Stress Testing, Stress Clients, and Market Research

When it comes to scaling your multiplayer game, choosing the right cloud services is one of the most important decisions you can make. But how can you make decisions without knowing the variables?

The key is stress testing through the use of stress clients and market research.

A valuable tool to create is a game client that can run headless, which automatically connects to your game server and simulates traffic. Stress clients can be an excellent approach for testing how your network code scales. It's essentially a DDOS attack of legitimate game traffic to see where your game servers start to take the strain.

Once you're confident in your game's net code, another step that can be invaluable in a pre-launch environment is performing a real-world stress test in the form of market research. You can perform real-world tests as a public test beta that runs for a limited duration. If you don't have a large following, you can employ a company like Game Tester, where you pay a large userbase of players to test your game servers for a set duration.

You can have a look at Game Tester's website over at the following URL:

```
https://GameTester.gg/
```

CHAPTER 7

Insights from the Masters

Sometimes it's important to seek inspiration from others, whether for motivation or understanding. Seeking knowledge from a master in a field can provide valuable insights and knowledge into a given topic.

In this chapter, I've interviewed some of these masters who've helped bring the games you love to market.

Let's take a look. First up, we have Michael W., the creator of Mirror Networking, better known in the community as vis2k. Then, we have Curt, a senior solutions architect who's been involved in games like Apex Legends and Fall Guys.

Michael "vis2k" W. – Mirror Networking

Michael W. is the creator and founder of Mirror Networking. He and the contributors of Mirror Networking are why this book and many games are even possible in the first place. A special thank you to Michael for taking the time for this interview.

Tell Me a Bit About Yourself and Where You Come From

I was born in Germany and switched schools when I was 15-ish, away from my friends.

I didn't have the best time, so I started playing one of the early Asian grinder MMOs.

Super fascinated by that virtual world. I met so many people. Wanted to do my own MMO ever since.

So, I started reverse-engineering MMOs and developed bots to learn and have some income. I got into OpenGL and Delphi, C++, etc. Made my first engine, always with MMO as the goal.

Little town and environment, couple of monsters, server actually ran stable for months at a time. 60ish CCU, not much yet. Realized productivity was not ideal in C++. 60k LOC for a simple MMO scene already.

© Dylan Engelbrecht 2022
D. Engelbrecht, *Building Multiplayer Games in Unity*, https://doi.org/10.1007/978-1-4842-7474-3_7

I studied computer science to learn more.

I got into Unity development when it was around version 4. Not worrying about renderer, animations, physics, multiplatform, etc. was nice. I kept at it, making some small games.

Meanwhile, I tried Java, Python, Clojure, Erlang, and probably ten other languages for the MMO server. I learned a lot, especially with Erlang. Still, the situation seemed not ideal.

On summer vacation in August 2015, I saw the UNET beta. I tried it; it was full of bugs, but server and client in one project, SyncVars, Rpcs, etc. It blew me away. I knew that this was the solution to the problem. It was super obvious.

The first thing I tried was their moving ball demo. I immediately started on uMMORPG.

I created health bars, monsters, NPCs, etc. UNET bugs were frustrating, but I released the first version in December 2015, hoping to make enough money to buy a pizza while developing sometimes.

It turns out many people wanted to make an MMO, which finally allowed me to work on it full time.

UNET is still full of bugs. I begged pretty much everyone on the team for fixes – nothing.

So, I ended up forking it to fix some of them myself, back when we still had to replace Unity.Networking.dll in the Unity installation folder. Weaver wasn't even open source at first.

That's how Mirror started.

It's 2021 now, been a while – thousands of bug fixes and improvements. The goal is to finish the roadmap this year, then maybe take a vacation and finally start working on my MMO.

Some people already have small MMOs running with Mirror today. It seems like it's finally possible.

I still want to remake the same MMO I played when I was 15. Maybe it's too late now, and people don't enjoy grinders anymore. But it doesn't matter.

I just have to do it for myself.

What Are Some of the Biggest Networking-Related Challenges That You and Your Team, or Clients, Have Faced While Shipping Multiplayer Games?

The biggest challenge was always to find an order-of-magnitude improvement in productivity.

Most multiplayer games never see the light of day because finishing the code is just too difficult. Luckily, Sean Riley made UNET, and a whole bunch of smart people made Unity. We are standing on the shoulders of giants.

Unity and Mirror were the answer for us.

I still love the engine architecture. It's just super easy to work with for my MMO goal.

For development itself, there are a lot of challenges all the time. There's no "multiplayer games course," let alone for MMOs. It's a lot of trial and error. Read, think of new ways, try, and see what works.

I am currently trying a delta compression algorithm from 1986, long before online games.

Mirror Networking seems to be the biggest open-source project for Unity. That was a challenge to learn as well. Every commit could brick thousands of people's projects, affecting hundreds of thousands of players. We have to be super careful.

Working with such a large community is interesting. So, many people contribute voluntarily, asking for nothing in return. It makes me speechless at times.

On the other hand, everyone wants Mirror to be something different, which has caused much friction over the years. I am still happy with the UNET architecture.

I just want to fix it and clean it up to make my game.

How Did You Overcome These Challenges?

"In the information age, the barriers just aren't there. The barriers are self-imposed. If you want to set off and go develop some grand new thing, you don't need millions of dollars of capitalization. You need enough pizza and Diet Coke to stick in your refrigerator, a cheap PC to work on, and the dedication to go through with it. We slept on floors. We waded across rivers." —John D. Carmack, Masters of Doom

What Would You Say Is Important?

User Acquisition or User Retention?
User retention
Should You Focus on Optimizing Network Code or on Cloud Infrastructure?
Optimizing network code

How Much Value Per Player in USD Is a Good Target?

Make a fun game. The rest will come.

What Is Your Preferred Cloud Infrastructure Provider for Server Hosting?

Google Cloud Platform

What Is the Most Crucial Piece of Advice You Could Give to Someone Learning Multiplayer Game Development?

I think Tim Ferriss said this:
"Is it an itch, or is it a burn?If it's an itch, don't do it.If it's a burn, you can't not do it."
Practical advice: **Look for orders of magnitude improvements**.

- Unity saves you 5–10 years working on your own engine.

- Server and Client in one project gives you 10x productivity.

- Using an existing networking library saves you years of headaches.

Open source is a big deal too.

Multiplayer games, especially servers, are supposed to run for long periods. For most of us, this is our dream project. Players live in that virtual world, meet friends, have guilds, get married.

If there's a bug, I want to be able to fix it.

I don't ever want to beg anyone for fixes again; it is terrible, soul-destroying.

Especially when in 10 years from now when I still run my game, and those people aren't around anymore. When using Unity, you are launching your game into a black box – hoping for the best. Doing so is a massive risk for multiplayer servers.

At least networking is open source now.

That matters a lot.

Someday, we'll have an open-source engine too.

Do You Have Any Other Advice That You'd Like to Include for My Readers?

- Eat healthily, don't do drugs, and hit the gym.

- Coding 80+ hours a week is hard.

- Train your body so it can keep up with your mind.

Do You Want to Thank Anyone?

- Unity. I love this engine. I really do.

- Sean Riley and Alexey Abramychev from the UNET team for making this possible.

- Paul Pacheco for his work on Mirror and pushing for tests.

- All the contributors.

- I want to thank everyone who helped out in the Mirror Discord.

- And the Unity Asset Store team for helping me to get my dream job.

Curt – Senior Solutions Architect

Curt is a senior solutions architect and a true industry veteran with 9 years under his belt.

Tell Me a Bit About Yourself and Where You Come From

I got into game services by administering Counter-Strike servers in the early 2000s.

From there, I applied for roles in the game industry, off the back of this, starting with managing servers for CS LAN tournaments.

I then worked my way to more robust roles, focusing on supporting online games and managing integrations of enterprise-level games with orchestration systems.

My skills grew to include matchmakers and related services within developer needs.

Now, I help to construct the end-to-end solutions of those backend services, leaning on my previous experiences.

What Are Some of the Biggest Networking-Related Challenges That You and Your Team, or Clients, Have Faced While Shipping Multiplayer Games?

Netcode. When I work with developers, the first challenge is always netcode. Every game is different, and as such, there are no perfect out-of-the-box solutions unless you are making an arena shooter.

The next is backend services asking questions such as the following:

- What dedicated server would you use? Unity headless server?

- What netcode/transport would you use: Photon Bolt, Unity MLAPI, or custom?

- How many players max would the game-server support? 30 or 3000?

- How would you allocate a game server from dynamic capacity, or would you not scale at all?

- What would make the allocation? A Matchmaker? Another service? How would you reconcile in use with available services and game servers? How would you manage these services? And importantly, who would support them?

Figure out your target network tolerances (RTT), 50/100ms/200ms, etc., and determine if the net code supports such latencies.

Decide how many clusters you would want to support worldwide.

How would you direct players to regional services; can they change regions manually?

How does the player flow (the loop, play game, repeat) look like in terms of backend services?

How is it secure?

How Did You Overcome These Challenges?

Typically, this comes down to my mantra:

Every game is different, and as such, you need to figure out what works for you.

Not all games have perfect solutions, and things change along the way. It's really about managing these solutions in a structure. For example, how can you ensure that you don't need to refactor the new code 3 months before launch?

You need to understand the areas you'll be serving, which would influence latency tolerances and help format the structure of the net code. It is a lot like the chicken and the egg, where publishing and release structure impact development and technology choices

What Would You Say Is Important?

User Acquisition or User Retention?

User retention

Should You Focus on Optimizing Network Code or on Cloud Infrastructure?

A balance between both, slightly favoring cloud infrastructure.

How Would You Go About Handling a Sudden Spike of Players? More Server Nodes or Login Queues?

More server nodes

What Is More Important in Multiplayer-Level Design? Balance or Map Fun Factor?

A good balance between the two, slightly favoring balance.

How Much Value Per Player in USD Is a Good Target?

$1–2 per player, PCM, and server hosting costs – that's concurrent. This value would become more complex if you need, as an example, a 40% margin since that player might only be online 10% of a month.

How Much Should You Be Spending on Cloud Infrastructure as a Percentage of Your Budget?

It depends on the importance; is it online only?

What Is Your Preferred Cloud Infrastructure Provider for Databases?

Azure for MySQL and GCP or AWS for other databases.

What Is Your Preferred Cloud Infrastructure Provider for Server Hosting?

Unity Multiplay

What Is the Most Crucial Piece of Advice You Could Give to Someone Learning Multiplayer Game Development?

The unknown questions are the most important.

Position yourself as the player as much as possible to find them. Users with bad network connectivity on their end will blame you for bad servers, as an example.

Make sure your game is enjoyable above all else.

CHAPTER 8

Challenge What You Know

The best way to learn is through practice. As such, I've curated some challenges for you to practice what you've learned throughout this book. These challenges will be split into three categories, and I'd encourage you to complete them in order.

Beginner challenges will tackle the basic intricacies of multiplayer development using Mirror Networking. Then, we'll move onto intermediate challenges, expanding on the previous challenges with user data persistence. Finally, we'll wrap up by extending the challenges further – adding world and user data persistence.

I encourage you to leverage AWS or Azure's free-tier servers to complete these challenges – this will help foster your experience with these platforms and be extremely valuable in your career.

I will lay out these challenges in a format that describes the challenge, the required conditions to complete the challenges, and finally, some bonus conditions if you'd like to challenge yourself further.

And remember to take a break, and don't burn yourself out.

Let's get started.

Beginner Challenges – Core Multiplayer Functionality

I will focus the following challenges on fostering your ability to create core, multiplayer functionality that will help relay game state between clients. You don't need to make these challenges pretty, so please use primitive shapes and objects if no art is available. We're focused on the multiplayer here. If you'd like to make it look a bit more polished, that's great too, but don't lose any sleep over it.

© Dylan Engelbrecht 2022
D. Engelbrecht, *Building Multiplayer Games in Unity*, https://doi.org/10.1007/978-1-4842-7474-3_8

Challenge #1 – Multiplayer 2D Table Tennis

Overview

In this challenge, you'll be modeling a game based on one of the earliest arcade games created. The game centers the screen around two players, each controlling a paddle, to hit a ball to the opposing player's side.

Missing the ball results in losing that round, and the game adds a point to the opposing player. Let's take a look at Figure 8-1.

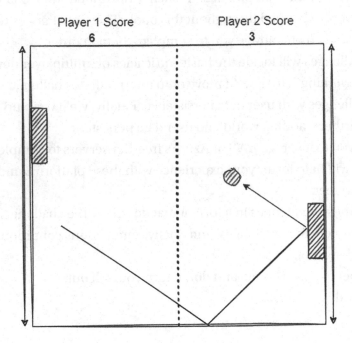

Figure 8-1. *The figure depicts a 2D table tennis game*

Depicted in red is player one's paddle, and shown in blue is player two's paddle.

Each player can move their paddle vertically at a fixed speed in an attempt to prevent the ball, depicted in green, from hitting their side of the wall. If the ball hits either the top or bottom wall, it reflects on it and continues to move. At the start of each round, the ball starts in the center and will head randomly toward a player.

Should the ball collide with a player's paddle, it will reflect off of the panel. To make things interesting, consider adding or subtracting an additional angle to the ball based on how close to the center of the paddle the ball was. Once the game completes calculations, the ball moves in its new direction with a slightly higher speed. This speed should get reset at the start of each new round.

The Challenge

For your challenge, I want you to recreate the game in Unity using Mirror Networking. Your game should meet the following criteria:

- Have the main menu that allows the player to do the following:

    - Start a new game, displaying their current IP address and game server port beneath the play area. The player starting the game should become the host.

    - Join a game, allowing the player to enter the IP address and port of another player's game server. The game should display a timeout message and return to the main menu if the player could not connect.

    - Exit the application.

- A round-based system that performs the following:

    - A round begins after a delay of 5 seconds.

    - Spawn a ball at the center that fires off in a random direction toward one of the players. IE. Not directly upward. Consider clamping the starting angles.

- Each player should have a paddle that they alone can control along the vertical axis of the screen.

- You should clamp each player's paddle to prevent it from moving out of the play area.

- The ball should reflect off of the top and bottom walls.

- The ball should reflect off of the player's paddle, with an adjusted angle based on how close it was to the center of the paddle.

- The ball should gain speed when colliding with a player's paddle.

- You should reset the ball speed at the start of each round.

- If the ball hits the left wall, add a score point to the second player and start a new round. Inversely, if the ball hits the right wall, add a score point to the first player.

- A round should end once a player reaches 10 points.

- The winning player should see a victory screen, and the losing player should see a defeat screen. Both players should disconnect during this screen. This screen should have the following options:

  - **Play again.** If the original host presses play again, it should start a new game. If the second player presses the button, it should connect to the details previously entered and connect to the host.

- The player's score should be displayed above the play area, relative to each player's side of the arena.

- The play area walls should be visible.

- Display a dotted line vertically down the center of the arena.

- Play a sound of your choice whenever the ball collides with something.

- Play a victory sound of your choice to the player that scores a point.

- Play a defeated sound of your choice to the player that loses a round.

Bonus Challenge

If that's not enough of a challenge, or you'd like to push yourself, try to complete the following bonus requirements:

- Create pickups that spawn randomly along the vertical centerline. Only one pickup may be present at a time and are activated when the ball collides with it:

  - Create a pickup that, upon activation, splits the ball into two, sending one ball in the original trajectory and another ball in the direction that the ball came from and counts as last hit by the opposing player. In this case, the round should only end when there are no more balls in play.

  - Create a pickup that changes the direction of the ball randomly, doubling its speed. Consider the ball last hit by the player opposite the direction that the ball is heading in.

  - Create a pickup that shows the ball's trajectory and subsequent bounce trajectory. Each additional pickup of this type during a round should offer an extra bounce display.

- Create a pickup that shrinks the opposing player's paddle by 25%. This pickup should reset at the end of the round.

- Add obstacles that randomly spawn in during the round within the middle third of the play space.

  - Limit the number of barriers to three and only spawn an obstacle every 10 seconds after the first 10 seconds have elapsed.

  - Collision with this obstacle should destroy it and reflect the ball as expected.

  - Prevent the obstacle from spawning on top of a ball.

  - If an obstacle will spawn intersecting with another obstacle, change the original obstacle's color, and require an additional hit to break the obstacle.

- Add an Escape menu that allows players to return to the main menu.

Tips   You're likely to encounter a few hiccups along the way, so I've prepared some tips that may help you during this challenge.

- Before spending time creating the game loop, consider ensuring that you have the network connection working smoothly.

- Vector3.Reflect() is an excellent method for calculating reflecting angles; you can read more about it and its usage in the Unity developer docs here: `https://docs.unity3d.com/ScriptReference/Vector3.Reflect.html`

- Build your game in windowed mode with a lower resolution while testing. Doing so will allow you to see both game windows simultaneously. You can do this in the Unity Player Settings, under Resolution and Presentation.

- Remember to ensure that your paddle logic only executes on the owning client.

Challenge #2 – Top-Down Shooter Prototype

Overview

Shooters and bullet hells are popular genres. I want you to build a simple top-down shooter for this challenge, supporting up to four players, with the first player becoming the host.

The goal is for your team of players to kill a hundred enemies with at least one player remaining. You should have a simple, flat arena with obstacles and a top-down camera that follows the player. The player should rotate toward the mouse at a given rate but not instantaneously. Players should move up, left, down, and right with the WASD keys, respectively.

Enemies should spawn continuously with up to 20 enemies on the map at a given point in time. Let's take a look at Figure 8-2.

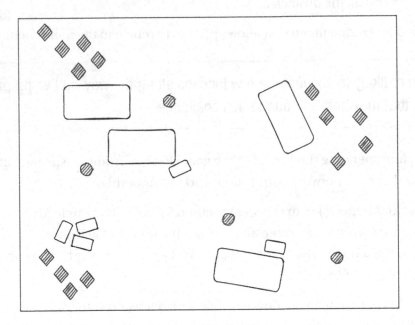

Figure 8-2. *The figure depicts a simple, top-down shooter*

Enemies pathfind toward the nearest player; upon collision with a player, that player dies and should no longer be able to interact with the game.

The Challenge

- Have the main menu that allows the player to do the following:

- Start a new game, displaying their current IP address and game server port beneath the play area. The player starting the game should become the host.

- Join a game, allowing the player to enter the IP address and port of another player's game server. The game should display a timeout message and return to the main menu if the player could not connect.

- Exit the application.

- Have a lobby menu where the host and up to three additional players can join the lobby menu should have the following functionality:

  - Prompt the player to enter a name.

  - Show all connected players and their ready status.

  - Have a button that players can use to mark themselves as ready.

  - Once all players are ready, the host should have a Begin Game button that begins the game.

- Players should spawn randomly at spawn points assigned around the map.

- After 5 seconds, enemies should start spawning in. These enemies should not spawn next to or on top of the player.

- Up to 20 enemies may be present on the map at a given point, no more.

- Players should start with 20 ammo.

- Players should be able to move with the WASD keys.

- Players should rotate toward the mouse at a given rate but not instantaneously.

- Left-clicking should fire a gun which will work as follows:

  - The attack should use a ray-cast system to determine impact.

- The attack should spawn a small cube with no collider at the impact that lasts for one second. This cube should be red if it hits an enemy or another player or black if it hits the environment.

- The attack should have a 1-second cooldown.

- The attack should consume ammo and not fire or go on cooldown if the player has no ammo.

- Hitting an enemy with an attack should do damage. When an enemy reaches zero health, they should go gray, leaving their object behind.

- Ammo pickups should spawn randomly throughout the map, giving 20 ammo to the colliding player. An ammo pickup should spawn somewhere on the map every five kills.

- Display the player's current ammo at the bottom right of the screen.

- If a player dies, their character, a capsule, for example, should go gray.

- The game should continue until no players remain or the players accumulate a hundred enemy kills.

- Upon winning, display a victory screen with the option to play again.

- Upon losing, display a defeat screen, with the option to play again.

Bonus Challenge

If you're enjoying this challenge and want to push yourself further, here are some bonus challenges to complete:

- Add a recovery system. If a player is dead, allow another player to walk up to the player and hold the E key for 5 seconds to revive the player.

- Add the following weapons, which the player can switch between by pressing 1–3 or scrolling with their mouse wheel. These weapons should not share a cooldown but should only deduct cooldown while they are active. The game should show the active weapon at the bottom of the screen:

    - The default weapon.

- A shotgun that consumes three ammo upon firing. The shotgun should fire three ray-casts in a small cone. The shotgun should have a 3-second cooldown.

- A grenade launcher, which lobs a projectile forward with some velocity. The projectile should detonate after 3 seconds, dealing a large amount of damage to enemies in the area around it. The grenade launcher should consume five ammo and have a 5-second cooldown.

- Add some basic visual effects for each weapon type.

- Add sound effects to weapons based on the weapon type, and adjust the audio position to match the player.

- Add a sound effect to the grenade collisions and detonation.

- Allow the player to sprint and boost their movement speed by holding down Shift temporarily. While holding down Shift, drain a variable called stamina, and slowly recover it while the player is not sprinting.

Tips

As with the recent challenge, here are some tips to help you out:

- Consider using a SpherecastAllNonAlloc to determine what a grenade explosion hits.

- Remember to ensure that non-player script logic only executes on the host or else you'll get some weird enemy movement results.

- You can use Quaternion.RotateTowards() to look toward the mouse at a given rate.

- Camera.ScreenToWorldPoint() is a great way to get the player's mouse cursor location in world-space. Use this in conjunction with the previous tip to help get your player rotation correct. Remember to lock all rotation except the rotation around the up axis. You don't want your player tilting downward or leaning weirdly to the side.

- Be sure to look at your movement code, and ensure that diagonal movement does not result in added speed.

- You can use Unity's NavMeshAgents for enemy movement or even player movement if you'd like. They're effortless to use. Check out the Unity developer documentation here: `https://docs.unity3d.com/ScriptReference/AI.NavMeshAgent.html`

- Remember to mark your environment as Navmesh Static, and bake your navmesh data.

- If you're struggling to spawn a prefab, remember to include it in the spawnable prefabs list. Instantiate the game object first, then spawn it.

Intermediate Challenges – User Data Persistence

It's time for something a little more challenging. We will focus these following challenges around user data persistence. I encourage you to use Amazon DynamoDB for these following challenges to familiarize yourself with creating applications with cloud-based user data persistence.

Challenge #3 – Chat Room App with a User Message History

Overview

For this challenge, I want you to create a chat room application. The goal is to have your application connect to a dedicated game server and prompt the user to enter a display name upon joining.

The user should see a list of all connected user display names, including their own in alphabetical order. There should also be a window for the chat. When a new user joins the chat room, the application should display a message in the chat.

You should store all messages and their sender display names in an Amazon DynamoDB database. Upon rejoining, the application should show the user all of the recent messages. Let's take a look at Figure 8-3:

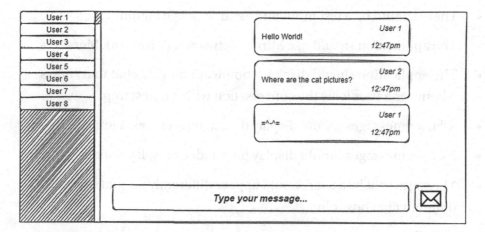

Figure 8-3.   *The figure depicts a simple messaging app*

For this challenge, we're not worried about security, authentication, or even best practices. I want you to solve a requirement that almost any online game has – the need for text chat.

Text chat is a core part of any online multiplayer game, as it allows users to make new friends, strategize, or just be rude to one another. If you're developing a multiplayer product, chances are, you'll need to know how to do this.

So, let's get to it.

The Challenge

- Develop a multiplayer application that allows for up to 200 connected clients using the Mirror KCP transport.

- Have the application automatically attempt to connect to the game server, retrying until a connection is successful.

- The application should have an Exit menu.

- The application should have a screen notifying the user that they are currently connecting.

- The application should prompt the user to choose a display name. Remember their last display name using player prefs.

- The application should show all users currently connected.

- The application should have a chat window for displaying the user messages.

- There should be a text input and Send Message button.

- The application should use Mirror Networking's Network Messages.

- The application should display a notification in the chat that shows whenever a user joins the conversation with a timestamp.

- All user messages should display timestamps of messages.

- All user messages should display the sender's display name.

- Messages sent by a user should appear differently for that user. IE. A different chat box color.

Bonus Challenge

Up for a challenge? Here are some additional tasks to complete for this challenge to push your understanding of Mirror Networking:

- Users should directly message other users in a separate chat window by clicking on the target user within the left user menu. This chat should also persist and be accessible between sessions.

- Allow for users to create a group chat. The group chat name should show up within the left user menu to all members within the group chat.

- Allow for users to choose an image file and upload it to the chat. You can handle this however you'd like, as long as the image persists between sessions.

- Allow a user to block another user. That user's messages should show up as "Blocked Message," and the blocked user should not have the ability to send direct messages to the blocking user.

- Ensure that your user interface can adjust to multiple screen resolutions.

- Deploy a build to Android, and have the android client able to connect to the chat. This Android client should function identically to the desktop client.

- Sanitize your user inputs to prevent breaking your database and application by removing TMPText markdown and glitchy ASCII symbols (see https://en.wikipedia.org/wiki/Zalgo_text).

Tips

This challenge is not as easy as it sounds and will prove significantly more challenging than easy ones. Do not let that deter you. Here are some tips to help you out:

- MessagePackC# is an incredibly powerful C# serializer. Serializing and then deserializing can help transfer data, like images, over the Mirror Network. MessagePackC# will allow you to convert practically any data into bytes, which you can then send over Mirror Networking. Once received, simply deserialize the data back into its base type. You can learn more, and download it from the following link: https://github.com/neuecc/MessagePack-CSharp

- Layout groups can prove helpful when building your UI.

- If your messages are larger than your transport layer's maximum packet size, typically, when sending serialized data, your message will fail to send. Consider splitting the data into segments, and reconstruct the message on the receiving end. Increasing the maximum packet size will result in your RAM getting filled, followed by your application crashing.

- Consider stripping out any code interacting with the database from non-server builds. Doing so may come in handy when deploying to Android.

Advanced Challenges – World Persistence

By now, you might be feeling comfortable with multiplayer networking, so let's take these challenges further and help build your experience with world persistence. These challenges will be significantly more complicated than the previous ones, but feel free to use primitive shapes, and do not worry too much about the visual appeal. We're interested in learning and practicing the logical side of multiplayer networking.

Challenge #4 – Farming Mechanics with World Persistence

Farming games are a popular genre of co-op play. Taking a look at the popularity of Stardew Valley and Slime Rancher, we can see that people love spending time acquiring resources and unlocking new crops or, in the case of Slime Rancher, slimes.

We'll be taking inspiration from Stardew Valley and building out some multiplayer farming mechanics for this challenge. The game should use a dedicated server that clients can connect to and authenticate with, where we'll challenge your usage of Mirror Network Authenticators.

The game itself should be a simple top-down game with a follow camera and use WASD movement. The player, which can be a capsule, should face the direction of the mouse and have an interface consisting of a hot bar toward the bottom middle of the screen. The hot bar should have nine squares, with the current selection outlined. This hot bar will represent the player inventory.

The hot bar should display the item currently selected. You can do this simply by showing the name of the item and the number of items that the player is holding.

There should also be a display toward the top left that shows how much money the player currently has.

Let's take a look at Figure 8-4 to get a better understanding of the challenge.

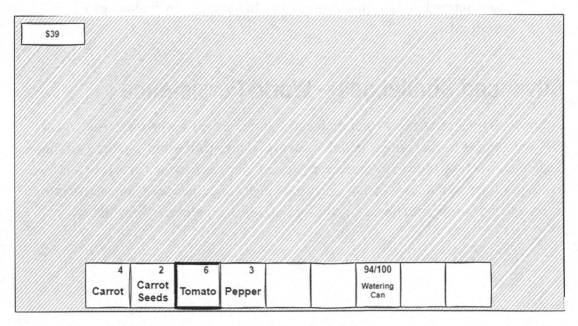

Figure 8-4. *The figure depicts the player hot bar*

216

There should also be an NPC vendor that sells seeds and buys crops from the player if the player is within the vendor's range and clicks them. Clicking on the vendor should bring up a small window with a Buy and Sell tab, allowing for player interaction.

Buying items should place the item in the first matching or empty hot bar slot. If the player's inventory is full or does not have enough money, the game should gray out the Buy button.

Let's look at Figure 8-5 to get a better understanding of the vendor trade window.

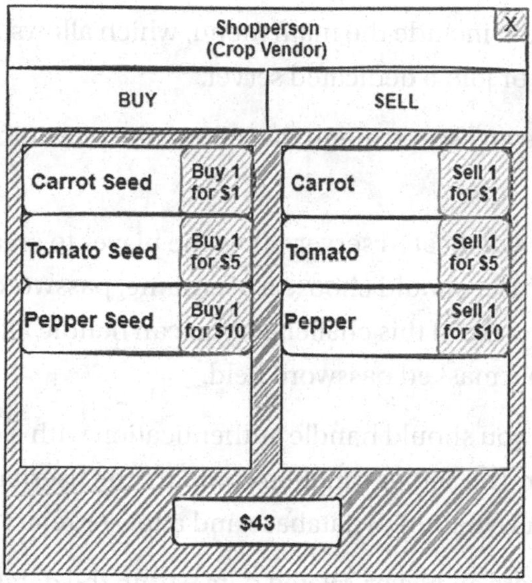

Figure 8-5. *The figure depicts a simple vendor trade window*

If a player sells a crop, the game should deduct one of the chosen crops from the player hot bar, and once the player has no remaining crops of that type, the hot bar should empty a slot. Players earn money by selling their crops.

With that out of the way, there's just one last thing we need: the planting, watering, and harvesting gameplay loop.

A player should select a seed in their hot bar and click Plant It into the nearby ground. Doing so should spawn a plant object that will grow over a few minutes. You should not be able to plant crops on top of each other.

Throughout the crop's lifecycle, it will consume water at a constant rate. At 30% remaining water, the crop will halt its growth, and at 0% water, the crop will wilt and die, requiring the player to "harvest" the crop with zero yields.

The player should have the ability to walk up to the crop and water it using their watering can, which they start with and cannot sell.

The watering can, can be refilled by using it on water. Using the watering can will consume water from the can and will need to be refilled periodically.

Crops that reach max growth will consume water at a reduced rate, and harvesting gives crops and seeds.

The Challenge

Let's break this down into challenge points:

- Your game must include the main menu, which allows the player to exit the game or join a dedicated server.

- There must be an escape menu that allows the player to exit the game.

- Upon joining a dedicated server, allow the player to create an account or log in. The user should choose a username, password, and display name. For the sake of this challenge, you can handle all logins using plaintext with a masked password field.

- During login, you should handle authentication with a custom Mirror Authenticator. The server can then compare the username and password to a DynamoDB database and allow or reject the client.

- You should store all player-related data within the database. Your data storage should include things like:

  - Player position

  - Player hot bar

  - Player money

  - Player account details

- There should be a buying, planting, watering, harvesting, and selling gameplay loop with all actions authoritative to the server.

- The game server should support up to eight players.

- Player display names should appear below the players.

- You should create a small play space for the game that includes:

- The NPC vendor

- Water

- Plantable ground

- Your game should have trade-with-NPC functionality built in, with authoritative server transactions.

- Your game should have player movement.

- Plants that the player plants should have their states synchronized and persist between play sessions and users in a single persistent world state. This data should be stored in an Amazon DynamoDB database and only interacted with by the server.

- Plant data should also be synchronized, such as water level.

- Mouse wheel or pressing 1–9 on the keyboard should change your current hot bar selection.

Bonus Challenge

Are you seeking more of a challenge? Here are some additional tasks for this challenge:

- Add some background music.

- Add a watering sound effect that plays for all players nearby when a player uses a watering can.

- Add three new crop types of your choice.

- Add a trellis structure that can be bought from the NPC and placed on the ground. Adjust tomatoes and at least one of your new crop types to require placement on a trellis.

- Add a fruit tree seed that the player can buy from the vendor. This tree should take a long time to grow, but it should give lots of yields and periodically give additional yields once matured.

- Allow other players to see what item a player has selected in their hot bar by showing that item model in front of the specific player.

- Add crows (which you can represent as a black capsule) that occasionally land on player crops. If the player does not move within range of the crow to scare it away, the crow destroys the crop, leaving a dead crop that the player needs to clear.

Tips

As with the recent challenges, here's a helping hand:

- You can use scriptable objects to create your item data. Doing so makes it easy to expand the game with new crop types. You can make a class serializable within a scriptable object by giving the class the [Serializable] attribute.

- Camera.ScreenToWorldPoint is a great way to get the player's mouse position in world space.

- To calculate consumption rates, you can use "remaining -= waterConsumptionRatePerSecond * Time.deltaTime" to reduce the remaining water relatively accurately by using that formula within the Update loop.

- Remember to sanitize any user inputs as they could mess with your database or game server.

- Do not save the plant and world state to the database every tick as this could burn through your rate limits on AWS DynamoDB. Instead, consider saving critical information like player trades immediately and saving world state every few minutes in as few database calls as possible.

- The saving and loading will likely be one of the most significant challenges of this exercise, and that's the point – don't give up.

- Consider using MessagePackC# for Unity, linked in challenge #3, to aid with your saving and loading of world data.

- A player should be able to harvest and water another player's crop; that's something to keep in mind when planning out your authority structure.

Challenge #5 – Box-Hoarder

I've designed the following challenge to push your usage of physics within a multiplayer environment, a requirement that many modern multiplayer games have, along with reinforcing your world persistence experience from the last challenge.

This challenge aims to create a first-person game supporting 16 players connecting to a dedicated server. The objective is to collect boxes within the game world and bring them to your claimed delivery point.

There are eight delivery points scattered around the play area. A delivery point contains a demarcated area, a Deliver button, and an indicator that displays the current owner.

The claim indicator is color-coded and shows the percentage of a player's claim on the delivery point.

If a player stands within the claim indicator, they begin claiming the delivery site. If another player controls a delivery site, they will receive an alert notifying them that a player is attempting to control the delivery site. If two or more players are within the claim indicator, the claiming process pauses until only a single player is within the ring.

Players can pick up a single box at a time, and upon throwing the box, it travels in front of them in a parabolic arc. A player needs to place boxes within a demarcated delivery point that they own and press the deliver button. For each additional crate within the demarcated area, the game multiplies their score for the given delivery. Let's take a look at the Figure 8-6 for a breakdown of scoring.

Crates	Score
1	1
2	4
3	9
4	12
5	25
6	36
7	49

Figure 8-6. *The figure depicts the scoring table for the box-hoarder*

The goal is to reach 200 points before any other player. Once a player gets 200 points or has the most points after a 10-minute timer has elapsed, they are declared the winner.

Let's take a look at how the demarcated areas might look in Figure 8-7.

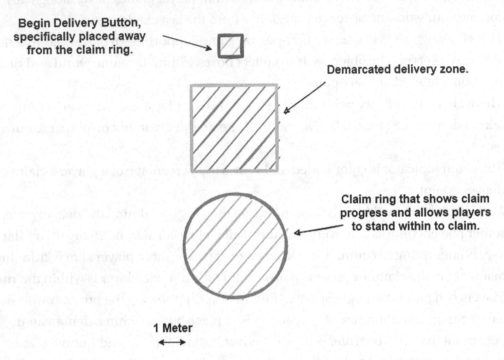

Begin Delivery Button, specifically placed away from the claim ring.

Demarcated delivery zone.

Claim ring that shows claim progress and allows players to stand within to claim.

1 Meter

Figure 8-7. *The figure depicts the delivery point layout in the box-hoarder*

We purposefully place the start delivery button away from the claim ring, and the player cannot complete delivery if anyone is claiming the current point.

The goal is to force players to either deliver boxes quickly or try to thwart the delivery of boxes by other players. A box should spawn randomly on the map every 10 seconds.

The box itself should be a networked rigid body that the player can pick up and throw. It should have a low mass, allowing the player to walk through it and push it around.

Let's take a look at the box in Figures 8-8 and 8-9.

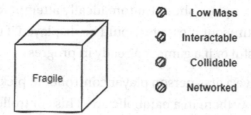

- ⊘ Low Mass
- ⊘ Interactable
- ⊘ Collidable
- ⊘ Networked

Figure 8-8. *The figure depicts the delivery box in the box-hoarder*

You should vary the arena itself where these boxes spawn with many barriers, walls, and obstacles. Let's take a look at what the arena could look like from a top-down perspective.

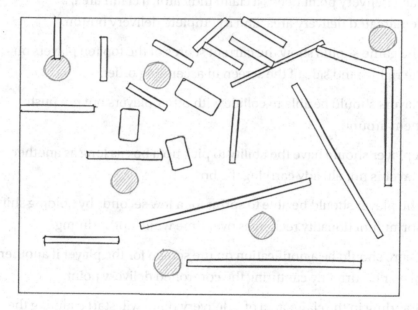

Figure 8-9. *The figure depicts a hypothetic arena layout in the box-hoarder*

The Challenge

The goal is to make the described game. Let's break the challenge down into the following:

- Your game must have the Main Menu, from where players can join a game or exit to the desktop.

- The Join Game option should prompt the user to choose a name.

- Your Join Game option should automatically attempt to connect to your server. A timeout message should be displayed if the connection was unsuccessful or if a game is already in progress.

- You should have a first-person player controller to pick up delivery crates and throw them in a parabolic arc. This controller should be networked.

- The game arena should spawn a networked delivery crate every 10 seconds.

- There should be eight delivery points around the arena.

- Each delivery point needs a claim indicator, a claim area, a demarcated delivery area, and a complete delivery button.

- The game should show the current scores of the top ten players on the right-hand side of the screen in ascending order.

- Players should be able to collide with other players but not push them around.

- A player should have the ability to pick up a box as long as another player is not already carrying the box.

- The player should be able to sprint for a few seconds by holding shift. Sprint functionality recharges over time while not sprinting.

- There should be a notification on the screen for the player if another player is currently capturing the controlled delivery point.

- Standing in the claim area of a delivery point will start claiming the delivery point for yourself.

- The game should end when a player reaches 200 points and displays a victory or defeat screen.

- When a delivery area is controlled, the controlling player can press the deliver button to deliver all boxes within the demarcated zone. Delivery cannot happen if another player is contesting the zone, such as if another player is attempting to capture it.

- When a player is within the capture zone, the capture indicator should display that control is under attack. Each player is color-coded, and the indicator begins to fill with the attacking player's color (Figure 8-10). If a zone is uncontested, the indicator appears gray or white. Let's take a look at Figure 8-10 to demonstrate functionality.

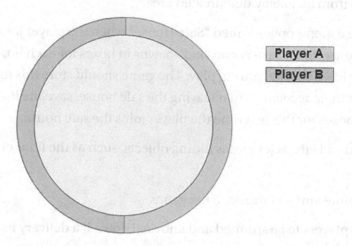

Figure 8-10. *The figure depicts a hypothetic point capture indicator*

- A notification should display on each player's screen once a player accumulates more than four delivery boxes within a demarcated area. We are encouraging them to steal the boxes.

- Players can open the Escape menu to vote to start a new round. If more than 80% of players vote, the server starts a new round, which will accept new players until there are 16 players.

- The arena should have no spots where a player can get stuck.

- The arena should not allow players to escape it.

Bonus Challenge

As you may have noticed, this challenge did not have a focus on the user or world persistence. That is due to the scale of the challenge. However, if you've completed the challenge and you're looking for something, well, more challenging, then you can attempt to complete these bonus tasks for the challenge:

- Create a basic login and account creation process when starting the game. The user should be able to store a username, password, and display name. We're not too worried about security for this challenge.

- Store information about a user, such as the number of crates delivered successfully, their playtime, and how many boxes they have stolen from an enemy demarcated area.

- Create a menu option called "Safe House" when the player joins the safe house, loads up a scene, and spawns in boxes for each box the player has delivered during play. The game should store this data within their account. When leaving the safe house, save the location of all boxes for the next time the player joins the safe house.

- Add sound effects for crates hitting objects, such as the floor or other crates.

- Add some ambient music to the game.

- Allow players to be stunned and knocked down if a delivery box hits them that another player threw.

- Add a minimap that allows players to see the layout of the map and an overview of control point ownership. This minimap should not show the location of players or crates.

- Allow the minimap to show how many crates are within each demarcated area.

- Allow the minimap to show how many crates are currently active.

- Allow the player to choose an untaken color, and save that as a preference to their account.

- Add the ability for players to jump.

- Add a more vertical map design that allows players to throw crates down several floors. Players do not take fall damage.

- Allow a player to carry up to two delivery crates at a time.

Tips

The following tips may prove helpful:

- You can use network authentication to send different custom requests to the server, such as querying information about your account. That way, you can build a custom authentication enum that states you intend to query information without joining. The server can see this request, validate your login, query the data, return the data, and reject your connection.

- Make use of Network Rigidbody.

- Don't be afraid to skip some of the bonus challenges. They may prove very challenging.

- If you're stuck on something, move on to a different problem, and revisit your issue afterward.

If you were able to complete these challenges, then you're well on your way to building multiplayer games in Unity using Mirror Networking. If you got stuck, then I'd encourage you to revisit parts of the book.

Multiplayer code is tricky, and sadly, there is no MakeMultiplayer() method yet.

The biggest challenge is getting into the mindset of multiplayer code. It requires a different way of thinking about challenges that, traditionally, you might find easy. There are many things to consider.

All in all, the best way to improve once you have a good foundation is through practice.

As such, I encourage you to seek out new challenges and come up with your challenges too; with that said, the most crucial part is to start small. If you come up with a monumental challenge that burns you out after a month, then there's no point.

There are many game idea generators out there. I encourage you to use them to come up with your challenges. Good luck!

CHAPTER 9

Where To Now? Conclusion

Thank you for making it through my book on multiplayer game development in Unity using Mirror Networking. I trust that you've learned a lot from this book and that it's helped to demystify the art of multiplayer game development.

The next step from here would be to practice your multiplayer development knowledge and decide what to focus on next. Multiplayer game development has a plethora of paths to follow. If you're looking to get into cloud solutions architecture, then it's definitely worth taking a short course, and hopefully, this book has provided some insights into which cloud provider will suit your needs the most.

Good luck on your journey; I'm excited to play your game one day.

A Special Thank You

I'd like to extend a special thank you to Michael and Curt for taking the time to answer my questions in such great detail.

I would also like to thank my partner for putting up with the many late nights I've spent writing this book and for the continuous love and support.

As well as my friends and family who've been so supportive, and to those who've been a bad influence, making me take a break here and there, giving my publisher gray hair.

Speaking of the publisher, I'd like to thank everyone involved in helping make this book a reality. A huge thank you to Deepak for doing the technical review and to Spandana and Shrikant for making the whole process such a smooth and exciting experience. You people are great.

And last but not least, thank you to all of the Mirror Networking people, the contributors, the community members – and the people over at Unity Technologies. I, too, love this engine.

Pave the way for your future self, the rest will follow.

—*Dylan Engelbrecht*

Index

© Dylan Engelbrecht 2022
D. Engelbrecht, *Building Multiplayer Games in Unity*, https://doi.org/10.1007/978-1-4842-7474-3

Printed in the United States
by Baker & Taylor Publisher Services

Printed in the United States
by Baker & Taylor Publisher Services